IMAGES
of America

ATLANTA'S
EBENEZER BAPTIST
CHURCH

ON THE COVER: The Men's Usher Board has served the Ebenezer Baptist Church congregation since 1946. Many of these men also were deacons and trustees of the church. (Courtesy of Ebenezer Baptist Church.)

IMAGES
of America

ATLANTA'S
EBENEZER BAPTIST
CHURCH

To Rodney Lytle

Benjamin C. Ridgeway

To God be the Glory!

Benjamin C. Ridgeway

11/17/09

ARCADIA
PUBLISHING

Published by Arcadia Publishing
Charleston SC, Chicago IL, Portsmouth NH, San Francisco CA

Printed in the United States of America

Library of Congress Control Number: 2009923608

For all general information contact Arcadia Publishing at:
Telephone 843-853-2070
Fax 843-853-0044
E-mail sales@arcadiapublishing.com
For customer service and orders:
Toll-Free 1-888-313-2665

Visit us on the Internet at www.arcadiapublishing.com

This book is dedicated to Sarah Reed, a member of Ebenezer for over 60 years, who served as secretary of Ebenezer Baptist Church for 50 years. Her notes and comments in the margins of programs and on the backs of photographs were extremely valuable in sequencing information and will be extremely valuable as an archives library is developed at Ebenezer Baptist Church. A devoted member of Ebenezer, she is the matriarch of a family, both biological and extended, that continues to faithfully serve Ebenezer Baptist Church.

CONTENTS

Acknowledgments   6

Introduction   6

1.   Beginnings   9

2.   Growth and Development   15

3.   New Horizons   85

4.   A Church for All Nations   117

Bibliography   127

ACKNOWLEDGMENTS

My thanks to Deacon Jethro English Sr., Rev. Dr. Albert Brinson, Shirley Showers Barnhart, Sarah Reed, Mary Gurley, Cynthia Terry, Howard King, Emma Bush, David Stills, Ada Slocum, Shirley Hider, and the editorial staff of the *Ebenezer: A Centennial Time Capsule* for the pictures and information they shared to assist me with the preparation of this book.

Unless otherwise noted, all images are courtesy of
the Ebenezer Baptist Church archives.

INTRODUCTION

A study of Ebenezer Baptist Church's history reveals a commitment to the church as an instrument of social change. Since Ebenezer's organization by John A. Parker, the spirit of service has been the cornerstone upon which the church has been built. Out of Ebenezer have come outstanding leaders who recognized that, as Dr. Martin Luther King Jr. stated, "in order to lead, one must be willing to serve."

While information regarding Rev. John A. Parker and Ebenezer Baptist Church at the Airline Street location is limited, the minutes of the Georgia Ebenezer Association do provide some history. Associations are groups of churches who meet together periodically for fellowship, denominational unity, and corporate ministries. The Ebenezer Association met in various sites throughout the state of Georgia. The 19th-annual meeting of the Ebenezer Association was held at Wheat Street Baptist Church in Atlanta, September 11–15, 1885. A review of the minutes cites the Committee on Business and Applications report, which lists the names and locations of churches that were by letter applying for membership in the Ebenezer Association. Ebenezer Baptist Church in Atlanta was listed as one of those churches. The committee report goes on to state that the letter was found sound in faith and practice and that Ebenezer Baptist Church was recommended to be admitted as a member. In the Church Statistical Table for the 1885 annual meeting, Ebenezer is listed with a "[N]ew" notation. The minister is listed as J. A. Parker. The clerk is J. H. Jones. The church had a total membership of 12. Reverend Parker also led prayer for the afternoon session of the second day of the meeting. Examination of subsequent annual minutes of the Ebenezer Association reveals Reverend Parker's continued participation with the association and Ebenezer's involvement in the association as late as 1904.

Two years prior to A. D. Williams assuming the pastorate of Ebenezer Baptist Church in Atlanta, the total membership of Ebenezer Baptist Church in Fulton County, according to the Ebenezer Association, was 44 members. When Rev. Adam Daniel Williams assumed the responsibilities of pastor of Ebenezer Baptist Church in March 1894, the membership of the church had dwindled to between 7 and 13 members. He did not allow this to discourage his determination to spread the gospel. Under his leadership, the small congregation grew and prospered. Approximately a year after he became pastor, his congregation outgrew the Airline Street location, purchased land, and built a larger structure on McGruder Street. Ebenezer Baptist Church continued to grow and, in 1900, purchased the church of the Fifth Baptist congregation that had decided to relocate. The wooden structure was located on the corner of Bell and Gilmer Streets. The church's outreach continued to expand.

The 37th Session Statistical Report of 1904 for the Ebenezer Association lists Rev. A. D. Williams as the pastor and R. H. Hinton as the clerk. The total membership of Ebenezer is listed as 461. By 1911, Reverend Williams was ready to lead his member to a larger facility. The property on the corner of Auburn Avenue and Jackson Street was purchased. Even with the dynamic growth of the congregation, Reverend Williams and the Ebenezer congregation reached out to those in need in community. With the prayers and support of his wife, Jennie, Reverend Williams brought Ebenezer to prominence in the city of Atlanta. His spirited revivals brought members from throughout the city.

From 1912 to 1914, the Ebenezer congregation met in a storefront building on Edgewood Street until the basement level of the structure on Auburn Avenue and Jackson Street was capped with a temporary roof. The congregation worshiped in the basement level of the temporary structure until 1921. According to the building permit issued in 1921, the estimated cost of construction was $40,000. Another interesting fact about the building permit is that there is no architect listed—construction was to be done by day laborers. The completion of the magnificent structure on the corner of Auburn Avenue and Jackson Street in 1922 symbolized the progress through faith, service, and dedication that the Ebenezer Baptist Church congregation had attained.

On Thanksgiving Day of 1926, Reverend Williams gave the hand of his daughter Alberta Christine in marriage to Rev. Michael Luther King. The newlyweds moved in with the Williamses. In 1927, as the church continued to blossom, Reverend Williams engaged the services of Michael Luther King as assistant pastor. Reverend King would later have his name legally changed to Martin Luther King Sr. Reverend King served as assistant pastor until the death of Reverend Williams in 1931. It was at this time that Reverend King Sr. assumed the role as pastor of Ebenezer Baptist Church. Reverend and Mrs. King had three children: Christine, Martin Luther Jr., and Alfred Daniel Williams King. Mrs. King, inspired by her mother's love for good music, invigorated the music department of Ebenezer Baptist Church. In addition to organizing a number of singing aggregates in the church, Mrs. King sought to bring first-class instruments into Ebenezer. One of the first such instruments was a two-manual Wurlitzer pipe organ purchased in 1940. In the early 1950s, Reverend King Sr. also embarked upon a building campaign that would add an educational building to the church complex. This renovation project, along with the installation of a new Hill-Green Lane pipe organ, would cost an estimated $250,000. Reverend King never neglected the social responsibility necessitated by Christian faith. He worked tirelessly for the equalization of salaries received by black and white teachers, voter registration, and justice for all people.

In 1960, Martin Luther King Jr. became the first co-pastor of Ebenezer Baptist Church. While by this time Reverend King Jr. was an internationally known civil rights leader, he was a son of Ebenezer. He was now the pastor for many who had sung with him in the choir, taught him in Sunday school, and gone to class with him at Booker T. Washington High School—the school for which his grandfather A. D. Williams was instrumental in gaining construction funds. It was at Ebenezer where Martin Luther King Jr. practiced his oratorio and developed his social consciousness. Along with his wife, Coretta, he brought to Ebenezer original ideas for fellowship through birthmonth clubs, fellowship hours after church, and a system of annual reporting to the congregation. His assassination on April 4, 1968, dealt a serious blow to the Ebenezer Baptist Church congregation.

In 1969, A. D. Williams King returned to Atlanta with his wife, Naomi, to become the second co-pastor of Ebenezer Baptist Church. In order to broaden Ebenezer's outreach of the gospel, Rev. A. D. King engaged the skills of his sister Christine King Farris to establish and later direct a 30-minute television worship service to be aired on WAGA in Atlanta. The program would air for over 20 years. Interested in providing for the youth, Rev. A. D. King also enlisted the services of Mary Manuel to establish a worship period specifically designed for children. The Children's Chapel she developed later became the Alfred Daniel William King Chapel for Children. It was the tragic death of Rev. A. D. Williams King that led Ebenezer to seek another co-pastor.

The third co-pastor of Ebenezer was Rev. Otis Moss Jr., who came to Ebenezer in August 1971. Reverend Moss led the process of setting up the Ebenezer Credit Union. He was involved with a renovation project of the Educational Building. His social activism in the Atlanta community also led to much of the desegregation of downtown Atlanta. The Otis Moss Chorale, one of the church choruses, was named in his honor. Although Reverend Moss Jr.'s tenure was only through December 1971, he had a significant impact on the congregation.

On June 30, 1974, Mrs. Alberta Williams King was killed during a Sunday morning worship service. A year later, Reverend King Sr. passed the torch of leadership to Dr. Joseph Lawrence Roberts. As the seventh pastor of Ebenezer Baptist Church, Reverend Roberts led the congregation from the Heritage Sanctuary to the Horizon Sanctuary. In March 1999, the congregation moved across the street to the new Horizon Sanctuary. In a time when many urban churches were moving to the suburbs, the Ebenezer Baptist Church membership chose to maintain its commitment of service to the urban community. Reverend Roberts provided stellar leadership to the Ebenezer congregation for 30 years.

October 1, 2005, brought to Ebenezer Baptist Church its eighth pastor, Rev. Dr. Raphael Gamaliel Warnock. He has energized the Ebenezer congregation to work toward "Victory in the Village" social action and evangelism in the community. The theme song of Ebenezer has been "Come Thou Fount." The second verse of that song reads, "Here I raise mine Ebenezer. Hither by Thy help I'm come." I hope that the this brief historical overview and the visual images shown in this book will give you a sense of the deep relationship that has existed between the pastors and the congregation of Ebenezer Baptist Church and an appreciation of the love, faith, and values that have through the years guided the church spiritually, morally, and socially.

One

BEGINNINGS

John A. Parker organized
Ebenezer Baptist Church and
became its first pastor. A small
box-like building on Airline
Street was the first home of
the Ebenezer Baptist Church
congregation. While there was
no fanfare or recognition at
the time of its establishment,
Ebenezer Baptist Church
"Stone of Help" (1 Samuel 7:12)
was to become a beacon for
those who sought to expand
the horizons of all people.
Reverend Parker served as
pastor from 1886 to 1894.

In 1855, Atlanta was divided into wards. Airline Street, Ebenezer Baptist Church's site of origin, was located in Ward Four. At the time of Ebenezer's organization, Ward Four consisted of working-class citizens: Germans and Jews to the north and blacks to the south. Before 1910, the ward had become almost exclusively black, centered on Auburn Avenue. The 1887 *Atlanta City Directory* lists Rev. John Parker as the pastor of Ebenezer Baptist Church. The church was not listed in the section naming the "colored" Baptist churches until 1900.

Cartographer Augustus Koch served in the Union army during the Civil War as a clerk and draughtsman in the Engineers Office in St. Louis. In his 1892 bird's-eye map of Atlanta, he shows a church on Airline Street [arrow added]. In the 2001 National Park Service's *Ebenezer Baptist Church Historic Structure Report,* it is stated that "it is likely that the church shown on the map is the original Ebenezer." As to the accuracy of the map, Koch was well regarded for his faithful representations. (Courtesy of the Library of Congress.)

Adam Daniel Williams was born January 2, 1863, in Green County, Georgia, to Willis and Lucretia Williams. He was licensed to preach in April 1888. In September 1893, he accepted a call to the Springfield Baptist Church in Atlanta. In the following March, he resigned that charge and, on March 14, 1894, became the second pastor of Ebenezer Baptist Church. It is estimated that the membership had dwindled to a range between 7 and 13 when Reverend Williams assumed the pastorate. The church was also heavily indebted. Under the guidance of Reverend Williams, the debts were liquidated, the dispersed membership reunited, and the congregation greatly increased. The increase was so great that the worship site on Airline Street could not accommodate the crowd. Consequently, land was purchased on McGruder Street to construct a new house of worship. The congregation remained on McGruder Street until 1900.

The Fifth Baptist Church was organized in 1871. In 1872, the land on the corner of Bell and Gilmer Streets was donated to Fifth Baptist Church by John H. James of Second Baptist Church, and a wooden structure was built. When the Fifth Baptist Church congregation decided to relocate in 1900, Reverend Williams and the trustees of Ebenezer Baptist Church purchased this structure. The purchase price was $2,500. The trustees making the purchase were James W. Johnson, Charles H. Eberhardt, Henry Edwards, and John Wortham. The church continued to grow in membership and popularity. Ebenezer congregants continued to worship in the structure on Bell Street until 1912.

Reverend Williams married Jennie C. Parks on October 29, 1899. She was the daughter of William and Fannie Parks of Atlanta. Mrs. Williams was extremely supportive of her husband's ministry. She led the women's groups and encouraged young ministers. In a biographical sketch of Reverend Williams, Rev. Gadis Ellington writes, "and he knows what ever may be his faults he has his wife praying for him. She makes him friends and holds them to him."

The Young Girls' Circle was organized by Mother Emma Clayton in 1918. In the center of this picture is Alberta Williams, daughter of A. D. Williams. Alberta Williams would later become the wife of Martin Luther King Sr.

Two

GROWTH AND DEVELOPMENT

EBENEZER BAPTIST CHURCH, ATLANTA, GA.
BUILT BY REV. A. D. WILLIAMS, D.D., PASTOR, 1921

Rev. A. D. Williams, D. D.

The cost for the Auburn and Jackson Street property was $5,750. A temporary worship site on Edgewood Avenue was used until the basement level of the church was complete. The basement was capped with a roof in the spring of 1914. The congregation worshipped in this site until the completion of the main sanctuary. Two possible reasons for the delay of completion of the sanctuary are the availability of funds and a devastating fire in 1917 that destroyed much of Ward Four. The building permit was issued on June 4, 1921, and, on June 21, 1921, the cornerstone was laid and the building was occupied in 1922.

Henry Charles Edwards, left, pictured with his brother James, was one of the early officers of Ebenezer Baptist Church. He was both a deacon and a trustee of the church. His son John Henry Edwards joined Ebenezer Baptist Church in 1912 and was later ordained as a minister by Martin Luther King Sr. In a handwritten account of the history of Ebenezer Baptist Church, Reverend Edwards refers to Ebenezer at the Bell Street location as the "church on the hill."

Sunday school was an integral part of the worship experience. Two of the women who laid the foundation for the Sunday school program are shown in this picture of the Ebenezer Baptist Church Home Department of the Sunday school. Pearl Reese, Sunday school superintendent, is on the front right. Emma Clayton, fourth from the left, was the superintendent for the Ebenezer Home Department.

Prior to the opening of Booker T. Washington High School, the primary option for blacks who wanted to attend secondary school in Atlanta was to enroll in the high school departments of one of the colleges in the Atlanta University Center. Because these were fee-based private institutions, many black students were denied the opportunity to get a high school education. Booker T. Washington High School opened in September 1924 and was the first public secondary school for blacks in the state of Georgia. The efforts of Rev. A. D. Williams and other pastors in Atlanta made possible the passage of a bond to fund the construction of the school. (Courtesy of the Atlanta Public School Archives.)

Deacon Jethro English Sr. is shown here with his two children, Jethro Jr. and Venetia. Jethro English Sr. was a member of the deacons board under Rev. A. D. Williams and is one of the names inscribed on the Ebenezer Baptist Church cornerstone of the Auburn Avenue location. Deacon Jethro English Jr. would later become the chairman of the deacons board. (Courtesy of Jethro English Jr.)

Pictured are some of the pillars of Ebenezer Baptist Church. They joined prior to 1906. Standing are, from left to right, P. O. Watson, Odessa Jones, Nannien Crawford, Emma Clayton, Carrie Bell Watson, and H. C. Edwards. Seated are, from left to right, Mamie Anderson, Amelia Griffin, Ella West, Sallie Mosley, Eliza Peek, and Cornelia Hill.

Michael Luther King moved to Atlanta from Stockbridge, Georgia, in 1918. After completing his studies at Bryant Preparatory School and serving as pastor of several churches in Atlanta and nearby College Park, King began the three-year minister's degree program at the Morehouse School of Religion in 1926. On Thanksgiving Day of that same year, King and Alberta Williams, the daughter of A. D. Williams, were joined in marriage at Ebenezer Baptist Church. The newlyweds then moved into the Williams family home, where they had three children—Willie Christine, Martin Luther Jr., and Alfred Daniel—within their first four years of marriage. Reverend King Sr. served as assistant pastor to Reverend Williams from 1927 to 1930. He assumed the duties of pastor of Ebenezer Baptist Church in 1931 following the death of Reverend Williams. Reverend King Sr. changed his name from Michael Luther King to Martin Luther King Sr. after his father's death in 1933.

Rev. A. D. Williams died on March 21, 1931. This stained-glass window in the Heritage Sanctuary is one of two gothic–arched triple windows. In the center, medallions are painted portraits of Rev. A. D. Williams (in the west window) and Rev. Martin Luther King Sr. (in the east window).

A list of names of organizations and members having made a commitment to having their names inscribed on memorial windows was posted in the church's 43rd-anniversary program, 1930. Among the churches participating in the weeklong anniversary celebration were Reed Baptist, Allen Temple AME, Travelers' Rest Baptist, Beulah Baptist, Wheat Street Baptist, and Big Bethel AME.

EBENEZER BAPTIST CHURCH

— comes forth with a great program combining the —

FORTY-THIRD ANNIVERSARY of the CHURCH
THIRTY-SIXTH ANNIVERSARY of the PASTOR
and MEMORIAL RALLY

BEGINNING SUNDAY, MARCH 9th
CLOSING SUNDAY NIGHT, MARCH 16th

This Church, Pastor and their work in the City, State and Country well deserve the keenest sympathy and fullest co-operation of the entire public. Every individual and institution of every description that have for its object the uplift of the people are asked and urged to lend the fullest co-operation to this program.

During these seven days, we plan to celebrate the forty-three years of existance of the Church and the thirty-six years of the pastorate of Dr. A. D. Williams. And plans further, to give a number of members and friends the opportunity of putting in a memorial window for themselves, family, loved ones or acceptable institutions. Every member who is not buying a memorial window is asked and urged upon to contribute to this great rally and anniversary occasion as follows: Men, $5.00; Women, $3.00 and members under twenty years of age, $1.50. Those who are taking Memorial Windows are as follows.

Rev. A. D. Williams	Mrs. N. W. Crawford	Dea. R. B. Hunter
Dea. P. M. Veasey	Dea. J. W. Johnson	Mrs. Victoria Rudical
Mrs. Amamda Hill	Mr. J. H. Reese	Dea. H. C. Edwards
Mr. Josh Googer	Mrs. Emma Clayton	Mrs. Amelia Griffin
Mrs. Fannie Daniel	Mr. J. W. Ward	Dea. N. P. Daniel
Dea. Henry Norman	Dea. P. O. Watson	Mrs. Odessa Hawk
Mrs. Minnie Dooley	B. Y. P. U.	Mr. J. H. Hanley
Missionary Circle	Usher Board	Choir
Sunday School	Deacon Board	Junior Church
Deaconess Board	Pilgrim Life Ins. Co.	Membership Committee of B. Y. P. U.
Hanley Company	Atlanta Life Ins. Co.	
Dea. W. M. Gibson		

On the interiors of the stained-glass windows in the auditorium are clear panes of glass that have been added to the face of the panels in the pivoting sash. The panes, which are not fixed in place, are inscribed with memorials in painted script and are simply slid into three-sided leaded channels affixed to the face of the original panel of stained glass (*Ebenezer Baptist Church Historic Structure Report*: page 57).

REV. M. L. KING, D. D.

Former pastor of Traveler's Rest Baptist Church and successor to the late Rev. A. D. Williams of Ebenezer Baptist Church. Rev. King's ability as a pastor is highly praised by the members of his previous charge. Being a graduate of Morehouse College and a real gospel preacher. This man of God is executing a genuine program of development which is bringing scores of members to all church departments.

Rev. M. L. King

EBENEZER BAPTIST CHURCH

THE LATE REV. A. D. WILLIAMS, D. D.

One of America's most outstanding ministers. He was called to Ebenezer Baptist Church in 1893. He began reorganizing with seven members and led them steadily onward until 1931. A remarkable record. Ebenezer's present magnificent structure was built under Rev. Williams pastorate. He has to his credit a full life of useful service and the distinction of being one of the race's best financiers.

Atlanta's Official Negro Yearbook 1932–1933 highlighted contributions in Atlanta. Black businesses purchased advertisements, schools provided information regarding students, and Atlanta's leading chauffeurs were identified. Churches throughout the city were featured. Ebenezer Baptist Church was one of those churches.

Midget Wedding Sponsored By Mrs W. M. Livingston
Atlanta Ga 1932

In the top center of this picture is the console of the mechanical tracker organ—one of the earliest organs purchased by Ebenezer Baptist Church. With a tracker action, the organist opens the wind channel by direct mechanical action: each key is directly connected via strips of wood called trackers and a mechanism called a roller board to the palettes that cover the openings to the pipes. The result is a very direct connection between the organist and the sound the instrument makes. The wind for the pipes was supplied by bellows pumped by hand. The pumper received about $1.50 a month for his services. The event featured in the photograph was modeled after the "Tom Thumb" weddings made popular in the 1920s.

The 47th Anniversary

Ebenezer Baptist Church
and
THE SECOND
ANNIVERSARY OF THE PASTOR
M. L. King

**Monday Night, March 19,
through March 25, 1934**

Church and anniversary celebrations were usually a week long, with church organizations taking leadership each night. On Tuesday night of this anniversary, J. C. Williams, the pastor's mother-in-law, presided on behalf of the Ebenezer Missionary Society. There were visiting churches and their choirs each night. The celebration ended with Grand Musicale performed by the then two choirs—Choir No. 1 and Choir No. 2.

The back of this photograph indicates that this elegant group of women is the Ebenezer Garden Club. These ladies were responsible for keeping floral arrangements in the church—especially for the two large marble urns, one of which can be seen on the right in this picture.

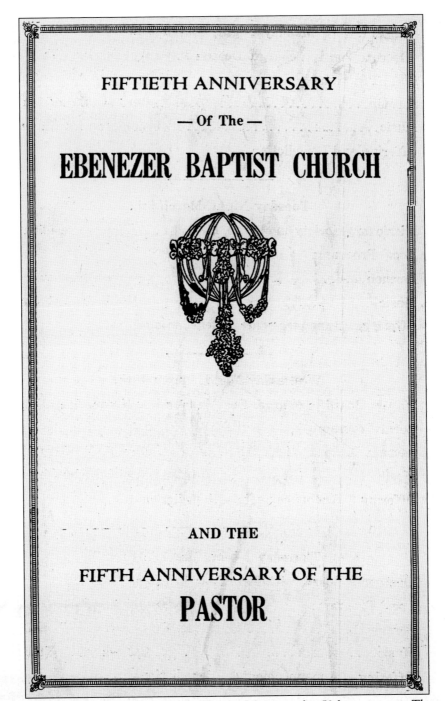

FIFTIETH ANNIVERSARY

— Of The —

EBENEZER BAPTIST CHURCH

AND THE

FIFTH ANNIVERSARY OF THE

PASTOR

In 1937, Ebenezer Baptist Church held a weeklong celebration of its 50th anniversary. The services were held Monday through Friday nights and were lead by various organizations of the church. On Sunday, March 14, the anniversary sermon was given by Rev. Noble Y. Bell, field secretary of the Home Mission Board for Negroes. Music for the service was provided by Choir No. 1. The culminating activity for the day was a musical program presented by Choir No. 1 and Choir No. 2 and Gospel Chorus lead by directresses Alberta Williams King and Carrie Wingfield.

Ebenezer Choir Scores At Gala 'GWTW' Ball

Big Bethel Choir Will Sing At Premiere Tonite

Tammany Hall In Harlem To Oppose Watson

It was the 60-voice choir of Ebenezer Baptist church, directed by L. B. Byron and Mrs. M. L. King, wife of the Ebenezer pastor, that drew long rounds of applause Thursday night at City Auditorium where the Atlanta Junior League staged its "Gone With The Wind" ball.

The trained choir rendered four religious numbers and each number swelled the hearts of the hundreds of lucky white persons attending the gay affair.

On December 15, 1939, the *Atlanta Daily World* reported: "It was the 60-voice choir of Ebenezer Baptist Church, directed by L. B. Brown and Mrs. M. L. King, wife of the Ebenezer pastor, that drew long rounds of applause Thursday night at City Auditorium where the Atlanta Junior League staged its *Gone with the Wind* ball. The trained choir rendered four religious numbers, and each number swelled the hearts of the hundred of lucky white persons attending the gay affair." (Courtesy of *Atlanta Daily World*.)

26

Alberta Williams King carried on her mother's tradition of creating a first-class program of worship through music. The purchase and installation of the Wurlitzer pipe organ brought a new dimension to Ebenezer's worship experience. The organ had about 2,000 pipes. The October 28, 1940, edition of the *Atlanta Daily World* reported, "The organ is said to be the most modern type available with a console consisting of 67 control tablets."

Rationing came to Ebenezer Baptist Church. With the onset of World War II, numerous challenges confronted the American people. The government found it necessary to ration food, gas, and even clothing during that time. Americans were asked to conserve on everything. With not a single person unaffected by the war, rationing meant sacrifices for all. In the spring of 1942, the Food Rationing Program was set into motion. Shown are some of the ration stamps and food certificates issued to Ebenezer.

The importance of maintaining proper decorum and courtesy can be seen in this picture. On July 7, 1943, Usher Board No. 2 met at the church to decide what the women were going to wear. They decided upon black crepe skirts and white celenese blouses. While the style of the blouses was not decided, the minutes from the meeting state that the skirts "are to have 10 gores." Also discussed were the proper procedures for handling various emergencies, where to stand, and the appropriate numbers of ushers.

There were many opportunities for members to worship and to serve during the week. This 1947 schedule of activities shows the many opportunities available to a growing congregation. According to the history recorded in the 1947 anniversary program, the membership had grown from approximately 600 to 3,700 in the 15 years of Reverend King's pastorate.

REGULAR ORDER OF WORSHIP

ORGAN PRELUDE
PROCESSIONAL .... Choir
HYMN .... Congregation
INVOCATION
CHANT
SELECTION .... Choir
RESPONSIVE READING .... Selected
SELECTION .... Choir
EMERGENCY ANNOUNCEMENTS
OFFERTORY (FOR MISSIONS)
ANTHEM .... Choir
PERIOD OF MEDITATION
SERMON
INVITATIONAL HYMN
ACKNOWLEDGMENT OF VISITORS
DOXOLOGY—BENEDICTION

WEEKLY ACTIVITIES

Sunday 9:30 A. M.	Sunday School
Sunday 11:30 A. M.	Morning Worship
Sunday 6:00 P. M.	Baptist Training Union
Sunday 7:30 P. M.	Evening Worship
Monday 6:00 P. M.	Missionary Society
Monday (after 4th Sunday) 8:00 P. M.	Deaconess Meeting
Tuesday 6:00 P. M.	Scout Meeting
Tuesday 8:00 P. M.	Ward Meetings
Wednesday 6:00 P. M.	Junior Choir Rehearsal
Wednesday 7:00 P. M.	Youth Choir Rehearsal
Wednesday 7:00 P. M.	Junior Usher Board
Wednesday 8:00 P. M.	Prayer Meeting
Thursday 8:00 P. M.	Choir I Rehearsal
Friday 8:00 P. M.	Choir II Rehearsal
Friday 8:00 P. M.	Teachers Meeting
Friday 8:00 P. M.	Ushers Meeting

Page 3

29

The Ebenezer Deacons Board (above) and the Ebenezer Deaconess Board (below) serve crucial roles in the life of the church. Deacons assist the pastor in visitation of sick and shut-in members of the church. In addition to assisting in the administration of the Lord's Supper, the deacons are spiritual leaders in the church providing the pastor support where needed. Traditionally, the deaconesses were wives of deacons or women assigned to assist with communion and baptism preparation.

Sunday school was a critical aspect of both spiritual and social development in the African American community. Ebenezer Baptist Church had a vibrant Sunday school program that offered classes for all ages. Note the number of children in this photograph. According to Jethro English Jr., former chairman of the Ebenezer Deacons Board, Pearl Reese would canvas the neighborhood singing "Bring Them In."

As the youth population continued to grow, choirs were created to give young people the opportunity to participate in the worship. The Junior Choir was started in 1950 with Emma Lyons-Hardnett as the pianist. The Youth Choir was started in 1961 and was lead by Claudia Butler Edwards.

Choir No. 1 was started in 1907. The name was changed in 1939 to the A. D. Williams Choir. I. B. Byron and Jessie Wartman were the directors. Notice the similarities of the hairstyles of the women in the front row. The women were probably patrons of the Co-Nell Beauty Shop owned by Nellie Perry and Corene Green, both members of Ebenezer Baptist Church.

Nellie Perry

Corene Green

COMPLIMENTS

of the

CO-NELL
BEAUTY SHOP

505 Irwin St., N. E.

Main 7460

— *Proprietors* —

SPECIALIZING in the SCIENTIFIC BEAUTY CARE of the HAIR,
SKIN, and NAILS.

"If Your Hair is Not Becoming to You — Be Coming to Us."

Master Operators

| Mrs. Auretha English | Mrs. Dorothy Haynes | Mrs. Louise Burnes |
| Mrs. Ruby Thomas | Mrs. Belle McKenzie | Mrs. Laura Henderson |

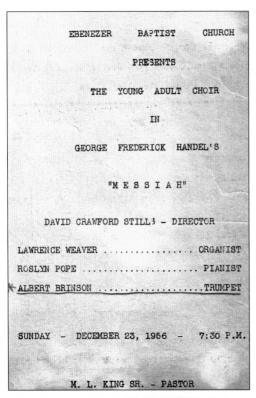

EBENEZER   BAPTIST   CHURCH

PRESENTS

THE   YOUNG   ADULT   CHOIR

IN

GEORGE   FREDERICK   HANDEL'S

"M E S S I A H"

DAVID CRAWFORD STILL3 - DIRECTOR

LAWRENCE WEAVER ....ORGANIST

ROSLYN POPE .... PIANIST

ALBERT BRINSON ....TRUMPET

SUNDAY - DECEMBER 23, 1956 - 7:30 P.M.

M. L. KING SR. - PASTOR

Ebenezer's choirs were among the first in the city of Atlanta to perform George Frederick Handel's *Messiah*. The Young Adult Choir was started in 1940 under the leadership of Prof. Earl Starling. David Stills assumed the responsibility of organist in 1950. The ushers are an integral part of the African American worship experience.

The ushers serve not only as greeters but also as goodwill ambassadors for the church. The ushers act as pages for the pulpit participants, making sure that necessary communication reaches the pastor or other pulpit associates during the worship service. The ushers collect the offering. At Ebenezer Baptist Church, there have been a number of usher boards consisting of a wide range of age levels. Shown here are the usher boards that served Ebenezer during the 1950s.

This choir was organized as Choir No. 2 by Alberta Williams King in 1932. In 1952, the name changed to the Martin Luther King Sr. Choir. The charter members of this choir are Auretha Jolly English, Jethro English, Anna B. High, Annie Thomas Hudson, Eula Thomas Manson, Frances Thomas Martin, Mary Anderson Remson, and Lillian D. Watkins. Anna High was the first president.

In 1956, the 20th anniversary of the M. L. King Choir featured Hampton Z. Barker, last on the right in the front row. The concert included Macfarlane's *Ho, Everyone that Thirsteth*, Rossini's *I Will Give Thanks*, and Dawson's *Soon-ah Will Be Done*. (Courtesy of Aleta Anderson.)

The Cherub Choir was organized in 1950. The director of the choir was Christine Farris. Here the group participates in an Easter program.

The Girls' Auxiliary was organized by the Woman's Missionary Union of Ebenezer Baptist Church as a part of leadership training for girls in the church. Under the leadership of Mary Manuel, girls are introduced to the social graces. Janice Colbert comes down the aisle of Ebenezer as the first queen.

CHRISTIAN EDUCATION BUILDING
EBENEZER BAPTIST CHURCH
ATLANTA GEORGIA
REV. M. L. KING — PASTOR
EDWARD C. MILLER ARCHITECT

In 1954, the Big Bethel parsonage, which was located immediately to the left of Ebenezer's sanctuary, was purchased for the construction of a Christian education building to house offices and classrooms. This letter from Big Bethel is in response to Ebenezer's request to buy their parsonage. With the purchases of this property and two others, the land necessary to construct the Ebenezer Education Building was acquired. The building permit was issued in November 1955, and the estimated cost of the building was $169,000.

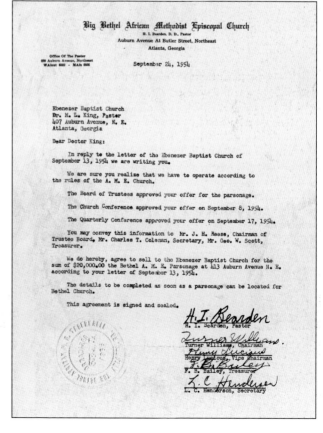

The dedication service for the Ebenezer Baptist Church Education Building was held on May 27, 1956. The building was dedicated with a sermon by Dr. Martin Luther King Jr., who was at that time pastor of Dexter Avenue Baptist Church in Montgomery, Alabama. The chairman of the Ebenezer Building Committee was William Nix, and the co-chairman was Jethro English. The contractor for the building was Barge-Thompson Company. A feature of the construction included a bridge on the second floor that connected the two buildings and gav the pastor and the choirs covered access to the renovated stage and choir loft.

On August 13, 1955, Ebenezer Baptist Church purchased an organ from the Hillgreen-Lane Company of Alliance, Ohio, at a cost of $17,800. The dedication concert for this organ was held on July 6, 1956. The guest organist for the dedication was Hampton Z. Barker, director of music at Morris College in Sumter, South Carolina. The organ program opened with George Frederick Handel's "Hallelujah Chorus" from *Messiah*.

DEDICATION AND ORGAN RECITAL........JULY 6,1956
8·30 P.M.   FRIDAY   8·30 P.M.

Ebenezer Baptist Church

Rev. M. L. King...Pastor

HAMPTON Z. BARKER_____CONCERT ORGANIST

The Hillgreen-Lane organ was a two-manual and pedal organ, having four divisions. These divisions were great, swell, antiphonal, and pedal. The instrument had 22 ranks, totaling nearly 2,000 pipes. The console was a tabulation stop key type, made of solid walnut. It was operated by 36 stops and 16 couplers. There were 23 manual and toe pistons. David C. Stills Jr., organist at Ebenezer Baptist Church, assisted in the designing and building of the organ.

This sign is probably one of the more recognizable neon signs in the country. Installed in 1956, it was a somewhat unique feature in outside signage of churches in Atlanta. Severely damaged in the ice storm of 1990, the sign did not work. As a part of the restoration process, the National Parks Service restored the white neon lettering and blue background sign to an operational condition in January 2002.

Funeral Rites
for
Mrs. Nannien W. Crawford

Ebenezer Baptist Church
Thursday, April 11, 1968 2:00 P.M.
Atlanta, Georgia

Rev. M. L. King, Sr.   **Minister**

Nannien W. Crawford served as director for the Baptist Training Union (BTU) for over 30 years. The BTU at Ebenezer was a part of Christian education designed to instruct all church members in basic bible beliefs and Baptist doctrine. It was held prior to evening worship on Sundays. Nannien W. Crawford was the first woman in the church to serve as a member of the board of trustees.

The Men's Usher Board grew out of Usher Board No. 2, which was organized by Mr. Alberta Williams King in 1943. The Men's Usher Board had its first meeting in 1946, and Clarence Mizzelle (pictured in the center of the first row) was elected the first president. Mizzelle joined Ebenezer Baptist Church in 1920 and was baptized by Rev. A. D. Williams.

The spiritual growth of young people has always been a crucial aspect of the educational program of Ebenezer Baptist Church. Children were expected to attend both Sunday school and Baptist Young People's Union in the evening. (Courtesy of Shirley Barnhart.)

Ebenezer Baptist Church was located in the midst of a vibrant residential neighborhood. Auburn Avenue was lined with two-story homes. One can get a glimpse of the corner of one of the houses in the background. (Courtesy of Shirley Barnhart.)

A Group of Baptist Training Union Workers

MISS MARZE BEARDEN, *Director*

Sunday was truly a day of worship in the early Ebenezer Baptist Church. The Baptist Training Union, BTU as it was commonly called, was an evening service that offered both a time of spiritual enrichment and scriptural teaching. Pictured here are some of the teachers.

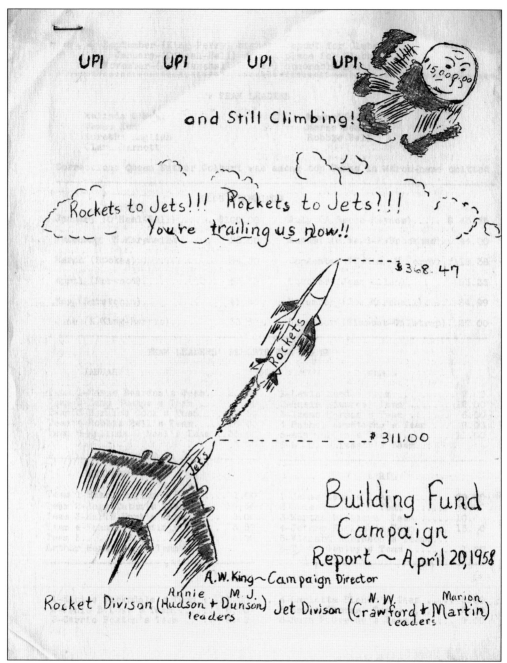

UPI   UPI   UPI   UPI
$15,000.00

and Still Climbing!

Rockets to Jets!!! Rockets to Jets!!!
You're trailing us now!!

$368.47

Rockets

$311.00

Building Fund
Campaign
Report ~ April 20, 1958

A.W. King ~ Campaign Director

Annie   M.J.   N.W.   Marion
Rocket Division (Hudson + Dunson) Jet Division (Crawford + Martin)
       leaders   leaders

Fund-raising had to be especially creative, because finances were often limited. This is an update giving a status report on a $15,000 building fund campaign. During this particularly competitive campaign, the teams reported their funds based on birth month, and each birth-month group was further divided into teams.

From left to right are Lonnie King, Julius Showers Jr., and Charles Green, pictured on their way to Sunday school. Sunday school programs often required students to use oratorical and dramatic skills. One of the young men pictured, Lonnie King, while a Morehouse student later participated in the writing of the "Appeal for Human Rights" that would lead to the desegregation of many establishments in Atlanta. (Courtesy of Shirley Barnhart.)

Style and grace can be seen in these three young ladies gathered in front of Ebenezer Baptist Church. The front entrance shown was changed in 1956. The young lady with the lean is Shirley Showers Barnhart. A third-generation Ebenezian, her grandmother joined Ebenezer under A. D. Williams when he came to Atlanta. (Courtesy of Shirley Barnhart.)

Minnie L. Showers stands at the door to the basement of the church. The basement was later referred to as Fellowship Hall. In 1914, the basement was capped with a roof and the Ebenezer congregation worshiped there until around 1921. (Courtesy of Shirley Barnhart.)

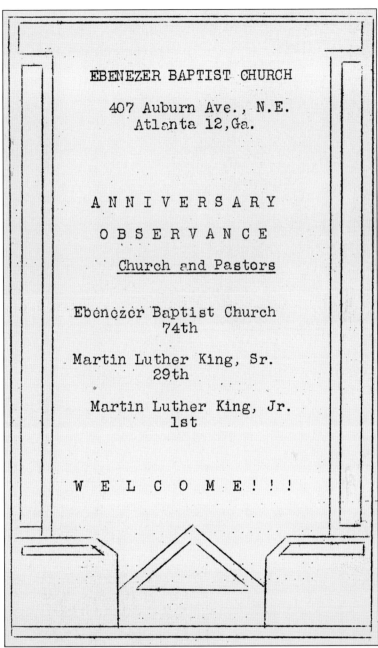

EBENEZER BAPTIST CHURCH

407 Auburn Ave., N.E.
Atlanta 12,Ga.

A N N I V E R S A R Y

O B S E R V A N C E

Church and Pastors

Ebenezer Baptist Church
74th

Martin Luther King, Sr.
29th

Martin Luther King, Jr.
1st

W E L C O M E ! ! !

In 1960, Martin Luther King Jr. was called to become the co-pastor of Ebenezer Baptist Church. Here Martin Luther King Jr. celebrated his first anniversary as co-pastor, his father's 29th anniversary, and the church's 74th anniversary. The Church Choir provided music for the service, and Dr. Martin Luther King Jr. preached the sermon. During the 3:30 p.m. service, the Ebenezer Youth Organization presented a *Tribute to Our Church and Pastor*. A combined choir, The Church, Concord, and Junior Choirs, culminated the day's activities in the 7:30 p.m. concert, "Evening of Music." Among the accomplishments of Dr. King Jr. during his pastorate were the initiation of monthly fellowship hour, publication of annual church report, and naming of a mission station in Africa for Ebenezer.

The board of trustees maintains the financial aspects of the church. The trustees were responsible for monitoring expenditures of the church and maintaining records of monies received by the church. Pictured here are members of the board who served in the 1950s and 1960s. Seated from left to right are Nannien Crawford (the first female trustee), Marion Martin, Mancy Brown, Robert Collier, and Reverend King Sr. Standing, from left to right, are Dr. George C. Lawrence (who in 1968 was given a full-time faculty position at Emory University Medical School), M. J. Dunson, and J. H . Reese (chairman of the board of trustees).

The Church Choir is a descendant of Choir No. 1, which was organized in 1907. In 1939, the name changed to the A. D. Williams Choir. In 1960, the Church Choir and the Young Adult Choir combined to form the current Church Choir. In 1961, the Church Choir had a roster of 69 members. In 1961, Hampton Z. Barker conducted the Church Choir in its annual concert. The organist was David Crawford Stills, and the pianist was Wilhelmina H. Stcretchin. Instrumentalists from Archer High School also the provided horn and percussion. The concert includes selections by Handel, Mozart, Vaughan Williams, Watts, Work, and Dawson.

Women's Day observances often included a fund-raising pageant like the one pictured. The queen was chosen based upon the amount of money raised for the church. This event was held in Fellowship Hall, formerly the basement of the church.

The Ebenezer Courtesy Guild was organized by Dr. Martin Luther King Jr. in 1960, shortly after he accepted the co-pastorate position of Ebenezer Baptist Church. The purpose of this committee was to assist in providing service to the members and visitors. The responsibilities included the sponsoring of a coffee hour each first Sunday in order for visitors and members to fellowship. Coretta Scott King was appointed the first chairperson of the guild. The original guild consisted

of 11 members. With the merger of the hospitality committee and the fellowship committee, the Ebenezer Courtesy Guild's membership was expanded to 38 members. Thirteen junior members were later added to involve the youth of the church. The guild significantly contributed to the social, cultural, and financial growth of the church. In 1967, Coretta Scott King relinquished her position as chair, and Lornell McCullough was unanimously elected to succeed her.

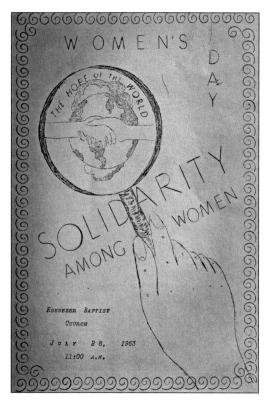

Women's Day is an important spiritual, social, and financial observance of Ebenezer Baptist Church. It is the annual culmination of a series of activities sponsored by the women. There is a financial assessment of members of the congregation, and the funds raised usually go toward some predetermined project or goal. Women take the leadership role in conducting the worship service.

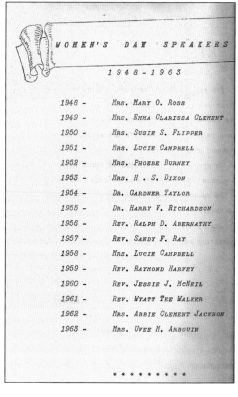

WOMEN'S DAY SPEAKERS
1 9 4 8 - 1 9 6 3
1948 – Mrs. Mary O. Ross
1949 – Mrs. Emma Clarissa Clement
1950 – Mrs. Susie S. Flipper
1951 – Mrs. Lucie Campbell
1952 – Mrs. Phoebe Burney
1953 – Mrs. H . S. Dixon
1954 – Dr. Gardner Taylor
1955 – Dr. Harry V. Richardson
1956 – Rev. Ralph D. Abernathy
1957 – Rev. Sandy F. Ray
1958 – Mrs. Lucie Campbell
1959 – Rev. Raymond Harvey
1960 – Rev. Jessie J. McNeil
1961 – Rev. Wyatt Tee Walker
1962 – Mrs. Abbie Clement Jackson
1963 – Mrs. Uvee M. Arbouin
* * * * * * * * *

This list of Women's Day speakers reflects the dedication to expose the congregation to speakers who are both spiritually and intellectually stimulating. Women also select a theme for the day, and the activities leading up to Women's Day are based upon that theme.

In April 1965, the Atlanta Board of Education voted to name Field Road Elementary the A. D. Williams School. Their justification for the decision was that "Mr. Williams was a Negro minister for 37 years and was Pastor of the Ebenezer Baptist Church for most of that time. He worked diligently for the bond issue that included the Washington High School." In 2002, in partnership with St. Luke's Episcopal Church and A. D. Williams Elementary School, Ebenezer Baptist Church embarked upon the I Have a Dream Project. This project identified 60 second-graders who would receive access to mentors, tutoring, and cultural exposure so that the students might be given the necessary foundation to successfully achieve a college education. The program was designed to trace the students from second grade through high school, and it offers college tuition to any of the 60 students who complete high school and maintain a certain grade point average. (Courtesy of the Atlanta Public School Archives.)

The Ebenezer Family solely
responsible for this Program

HONORING OUR SON

IN THIS HIS SHINING HOUR

A W A R D E D

THE NOBEL PEACE PRIZE

December 10, 1964 in Oslo, Norway.

* * * * * * * * * * * * * * * * * * *

MERRY CHRISTMAS TO ALL

AND TO ALL GOODNIGHT.

Mrs. Georgie W. Thornton, General Chairman

Mrs. Laura Henderson, Assistant Chairman

Mrs. N. W. Crawford, Co-ordinator

Ebenezer Salutes It's Son

DR. MARTIN LUTHER KING, JR.

8:00 P.M.

Friday   December 18, 1964

Fellowship Hall

Ebenezer Baptist Church

Atlanta, Ga.

Ministers

Martin Luther King, Sr.
Martin Luther King, Jr.

The Ebenezer Baptist Church family is a true family. It is a family that weeps together and celebrates together. A great example of this love is evident in this salute to Dr. Martin Luther King Jr. after he was awarded the Nobel Peace Prize. The program included musical selections, an Ebenezer choral reading composed by George W. Thorton and led by Carl Dukes titled *Ballad for a Great Man,* and other special presentations.

Ebenezer Baptist Church has demonstrated a commitment to the involvement of young people in the activities of the church. Here the youth prepare for Youth Week, a weeklong observance. Under the leadership of assistant minister and youth advisor Albert Brinson, pictured in the second row standing on the right, young people were provided opportunities to develop leadership skills that would be useful both inside and outside of the church.

In 1962, Marie Hunter presented the idea of an Ebenezer Baptist Church Youth Usher Board to Reverend King Sr. He approved the idea, and the Youth Usher Board was formed. The board started with approximately 30 members ranging in age from 13 to 15. Louise Bell was the first president. A few years later, the board became the Young Adult Board and then the Marie Hunter Usher Board.

In 1948, Usher Board No. 2 was renamed the Ladies Usher Board. Katherine King was appointed president. She served in that position for 25 years. In 1968, Ada Slocum was appointed president, and Katherine King became president emeritus.

The Senior Usher Board organized in 1922 during the pastorate of Rev. A. D. Williams. This board engaged the services of both men and women and served the newly completed second story of the Auburn and Jackson Streets church. The first president was Tom Lazenby.

On Friday, May 7, 1965, the women of Ebenezer Baptist Church sponsored Coretta Scott King in a performance called the Freedom Concert. The Freedom Concert was the story of the freedom movement told in narration, song, and poetry. The Freedom Concert series was a method used to raise money to support the civil rights movement.

An <u>Unusual</u> Type of Concert!

SOUTHERN
CHRISTIAN
LEADERSHIP
CONFERENCE

Presents

Mrs. Coretta Scott King
(Mrs. Martin Luther King, Jr.)
— Soprano —

Mrs. Coretta Scott King

IN

A 'FREEDOM CONCERT'

Sponsored By:
"The Women Of Ebenezer"

SCRIPTURE
"Behold how good and how pleasant it is for brethren to dwell together in Unity."
Psalms 133:1

Sunday   March 3, 1968
Morning Worship   Ten Forty-Five

MARCH- "CHURCH ANNIVERSARY MONTH"

E SERVICE OF PRAISE
The Prelude
*The Processional Hymn No.54-
                        God Of Our Fathers
The Invocation
WORD OF GOD
he Responsive Reading No.25 -"The Testimor
                        Of The Redeemed"
The Gloria Patri
he Choral Worship .... Glory Hallelujah
he Pastoral Prayer
he Chant No.530 ....Hear Our Prayer
The Hymn of Praise ...... Lord, Revive Us
EXERCISE OF CHRISTIAN STEWARDSHIP
he Prayer of Thanksgiving
he Anthem - Praise The Lord..A.Randegger
he Presentation of Tithes and Offerings
The Doxology
PRESENTATION OF THE WORD
he Meditation Period-If I Can Help Somebod
he Sermon...Dr. Martin Luther King, Jr.
RESPONSE OF FAITH
he Hymn of Invitation No.248-
                        Almost Persuaded
The Closing Hymn No.27.....Saviour, Again
e Benediction and Choral Amen
*The Postlude -

    *The congregation stands
    **The congregation is seated

        MUSIC FOR THE DAY
5 A.M. ..The Church and Concord Choirs
0 P.M. ....The Hymn Choir
            Ministers of Music
d C. Stills   Joseph A. Stephens
Alberta W. King .. Director-Hymn Choir

LORD, REVIVE US

Saviour visit Thy plantation
Grant us Lord a gracious reign
All will come to desolation
Unless thou return again.
            Chorus
Lord, revive us, Lord, revive us,
All our help must come from Thee.
Lord, revive us, Lord, revive us,
All our help must come from Thee.
            -2-
Keep no longer at a distance
Shine upon us from on high.
Lest, for want of Thine assistance
Every plant should droop and die.
            -3-
Let our mutual love be fervent
Make us prevalent in prayers.
Let each one esteemed thy servant
Shun the world's bewitching snares.

MEETINGS FOLLOWING MORNING WORSHIP:

Mission Circle #1 - R.103
Mrs. Minnie Gibson, Chairman

Mission Circle #5 -373 Felton Dr.NE
Mesdames Mary Perry and Mamie Atkins
Co-hostesses. Mrs. Fannie L.Roberson,Chmn

NEW MEMBER ADDED TO OUR FELLOWSHIP-Feb.25:

BY BAPTISM

    Master Raymond Boykin (Sept)799-3568
    664 Bolton Rd. NW

CHURCH ANNIVERSARY ASSESSMENTS:

    $6.00 per member to be paid through
    your Month Club. Children at least
                $1.00

The anniversary-month theme for 1968 was "Meeting the Challenge of the Times." Dr. Martin King Jr. preached the sermon during the 10:45 a.m. service on March 3, 1968.

TRIPLE ANNIVERSARY CELEBRATION

EBENEZER BAPTIST CHURCH

EIGHTY - FIRST YEAR

MINISTERS

Dr. Martin Luther King Sr.   Dr. Martin Luther King Jr.

Friday- March 15, 1968 . . . . . Sunday - March 17, 1968

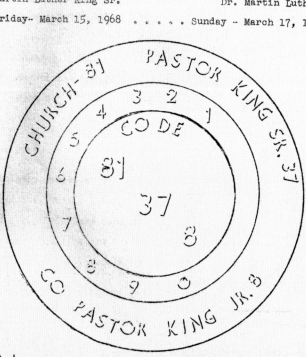

THEME: MEETING THE CHALLENGE OF THE TIMES

THEME HYMN . . . C O M E   T H O U   F O U N T

" Hither To Hath The Lord Helped Us "

A T L A N T A , G E O R G I A

The 81st anniversary of Ebenezer Baptist Church on March 17, 1968, was a packed day. The 9:30 a.m. church school program featured all the departments of the Sunday school. The 10:45 a.m. anniversary observance featured Rev. Joseph E. Lowery, pastor of the St. Paul Methodist Church in Birmingham, Alabama. The anthem sung by the Ebenezer Church Choir during the service was Rossini's *I Will Give Thanks*. At 3:00 p.m., the youth presented a program highlighting "The Dream of Those Who Blazed the Trail." The sermon for the evening service was delivered by Rev. Emory R. Searcy, pastor of the Mount Zion Second Baptist Church in Atlanta. The anniversary assessment for adults was $6 and $1 for children.

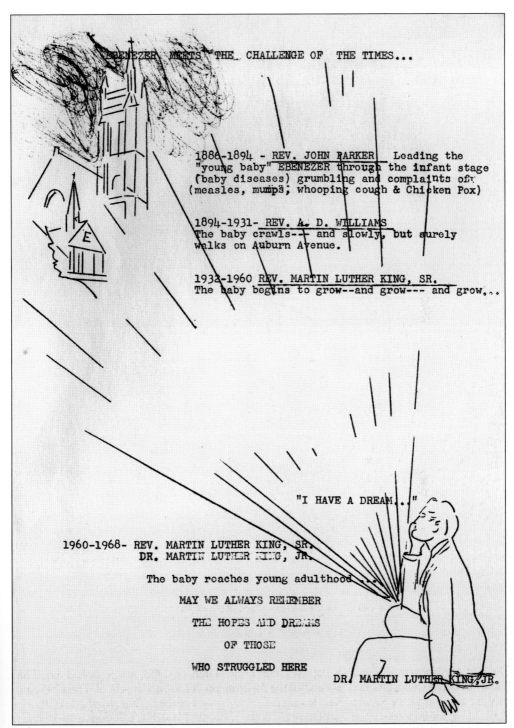

EBENEZER MEETS THE CHALLENGE OF THE TIMES...

1886-1894 - REV. JOHN PARKER   Leading the
"young baby" EBENEZER through the infant stage
(baby diseases) grumbling and complaints of:
(measles, mumps, whooping cough & Chicken Pox)

1894-1931- REV. A. D. WILLIAMS
The baby crawls-- and slowly, but surely
walks on Auburn Avenue.

1932-1960 REV. MARTIN LUTHER KING, SR.
The baby begins to grow--and grow--- and grow...

"I HAVE A DREAM..."

1960-1968- REV. MARTIN LUTHER KING, SR.
        DR. MARTIN LUTHER KING, JR.

The baby reaches young adulthood...

MAY WE ALWAYS REMEMBER

THE HOPES AND DREAMS

OF THOSE

WHO STRUGGLED HERE

DR. MARTIN LUTHER KING, JR.

This symbolic drawing depicting Ebenezer's historical development appeared on the last page of Ebenezer's 81st-anniversary program. "Ebenezer meets the challenge of the times." Only a few weeks later, Ebenezer Baptist Church would be faced with the assassination of its pastor, Dr. Martin Luther King Jr.

Obsequies
Martin Luther King Jr.

TUESDAY, APRIL 9, 1968
10:30 A.M.
Ebenezer Baptist Church
2:00 P.M.
The Campus of Morehouse College
ATLANTA, GEORGIA

When the world lost Dr. Martin Luther King Jr. to an assassin's bullet on April 4, 1968, Ebenezer Baptist Church lost much more. To his congregation, a pastor was lost. To those who knew "M. L." closely, they lost a friend and brother.

With the Reverend Ralph David Abernathy officiating, his memorial service included excerpts from some of his sermon. Printed in his funeral program are words from his February 4, 1968, sermon. He said, "I want you to say that I tried to love and serve humanity." This aerial view of Ebenezer Baptist Church on the day of Dr. King Jr.'s funeral shows how the single-family dwellings that had once surrounded the church had been demolished. (Courtesy of the Atlanta History Center.)

Ebenezer Baptist Church members frequently used drama to communicate the message of God's love and grace. This production, *Christianity in a Crisis*, presented in June 1968, dramatizes how through faith the challenges of life can be met and overcome.

Fun and food were common elements used to raise funds for church projects. In the example "Around the World in Eighty Dresses," the Young Women's Fellowship makes use of a fashion show. Notice the $1 for adult and 75¢ for children admission fees.

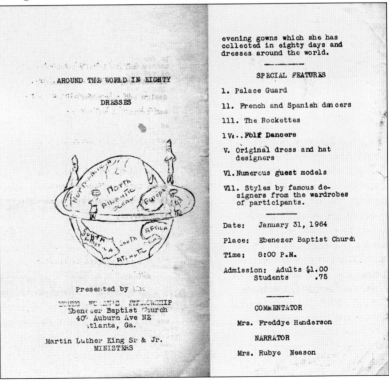

AROUND THE WORLD IN EIGHTY

DRESSES

Presented by the

YOUNG WOMEN'S FELLOWSHIP
Ebenezer Baptist Church
407 Auburn Ave NE
Atlanta, Ga.

Martin Luther King Sr & Jr.
MINISTERS

evening gowns which she has collected in eighty days and dresses around the world.

SPECIAL FEATURES

1. Palace Guard

11. French and Spanish dancers

111. The Rockettes

1V:..Folk Dancers

V. Original dress and hat designers

VI. Numerous guest models

V11. Styles by famous designers from the wardrobes of participants.

Date: January 31, 1964

Place: Ebenezer Baptist Church

Time: 8:00 P.M.

Admission: Adults $1.00
            Students   .75

COMMENTATOR

Mrs. Freddye Henderson

NARRATOR

Mrs. Rubye Neason

The stained-glass circular image depicting Jesus at Gethsemane was installed in the mid-1950s by the Llorens Stained Glass Company. Joseph V. Llorens Sr. began the company in Atlanta in 1921. The baptismal pool behind the curtain under the circular window was also an addition to the original structure. The two large pink marble urns were donated to the church due to the efforts of Nannien Crawford, general director of the Baptist Training Union.

COMMEMORATION SERVICES
for
Dr. Martin Luther King Jr.

january 15, 1929 -
april 4, 1968

FORTIETH

BIRTHDAY ANNIVERSARY

Wednesday, January 15, 1969
Atlanta, Georgia

The first service of commemoration for Dr. Martin Luther King Jr. was held on January 15, 1969. Rev. Ralph David Abernathy, president of the Southern Christian Leadership Conference and pastor of West Hunter Baptist Church, was the keynote speaker. The service also included music by Ebenezer's Concord Choir and soloist Mary Gurley. Rev. Alfred Daniel Williams King, now co-pastor of Ebenezer Baptist Church with his father, also made remarks.

Alfred Daniel Williams King was the youngest son of Martin Sr. and Alberta Williams King. He was born on July 30, 1930. He served as pastor of three churches prior to returning to Ebenezer Baptist Church as co-pastor in 1968. Reverend King, like his brother, was a minister who used his pulpit to address the message of peace, nonviolence, and social justice.

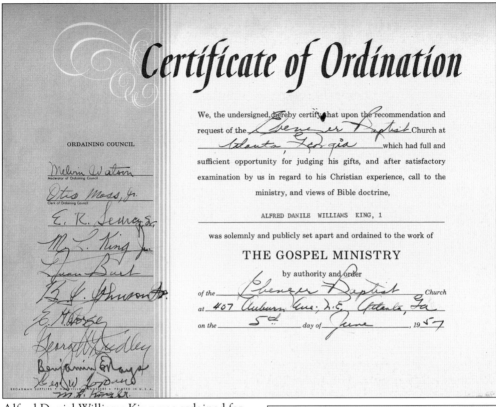

Certificate of Ordination

ORDAINING COUNCIL

Melvin Watson
Moderator of Ordaining Council

Otis Moss, Jr.
Clerk of Ordaining Council

E. K. Leurey Sr.

M. L. King Jr.

Juan Burt

B. J. Johnson Jr.

E. H Dorsey

George W. Dudley

Benjamin Mays

Geo. W. Jordan

M. L. King Sr.

We, the undersigned, hereby certify that upon the recommendation and request of the _Ebenezer Baptist_ Church at _Atlanta, Georgia_ which had full and sufficient opportunity for judging his gifts, and after satisfactory examination by us in regard to his Christian experience, call to the ministry, and views of Bible doctrine,

ALFRED DANILE WILLIAMS KING, 1

was solemnly and publicly set apart and ordained to the work of

THE GOSPEL MINISTRY

by authority and order of the _Ebenezer Baptist_ Church at _407 Auburn Ave. N.E. Atlanta, Ga._ on the _5d_ day of _June_, 19_57_

BROADMAN SUPPLIES • NASHVILLE, TENNESSEE • PRINTED IN U.S.A.

Alfred Daniel Williams King was ordained for Christian ministry on June 5, 1957. The moderator of his ordination council was Rev. Melvin Watson, and the clerk for the council was Rev. Otis Moss Jr. In that same year, Reverend King accepted the pastorate of Mount Vernon Baptist Church in Newnan, Georgia.

EBENEZER BAPTIST CHURCH

407 Auburn Avenue, N. E.   MUrray 8-7263

"Hither to hath the Lord helped us"

DR. MARTIN LUTHER KING, SR., Pastor
REV. A. D. WILLIAMS KING, Assistant Pastor

In 1958, as indicated on the front of the church bulletin, the Reverend A. D. King served as assistant pastor of Ebenezer Baptist Church until he accepted the call to pastor First Baptist Church of Ensley in Birmingham, Alabama, in 1961.

```
                    INSTALLATION BANQUET
                          for
            REV. A. D. WILLIAMS KING AS FIFTH PASTOR
             Ebenezer Baptist Church - Atlanta, Georgia

                  Matador Room - Paschal's Motor Hotel

Monday                   November 4, 1968                    7:30 P.M.

           *****  Mr. Ray McIver, Toastmaster   *****

Music .................................... Mr. Joseph A. Stephens

Invocation ................................... Rev. Austin Ford
            Director: Emmaus House - Atlanta, Ga.

D I N N E R

Solo .................................... Mrs. Jimmie Thomas

Greetings ............................ Dr. Hugh Gloster, President
            Morehouse College - Atlanta, Georgia

Music .................................... The Male Choraliers
                 Ebenezer Baptist Church

Greetings and Introduction of Speaker .. Mrs. Wilhelmina H. Scretchin
          Chairman: Installation Committee

SPEAKER ............................. REV. LEO LESSER, JR., PASTOR
          Lee Chapel A.M.E. Church - Nashville, Tennessee

Solo .................................... Mrs. Jimmie Thomas

Presentation - .

Remarks .................... ....... Rev. Martin Luther King, Sr.
             Co-Pastor: Ebenezer Baptist Church

Remarks - Honorees .............. Rev. and Mrs. A. D. Williams King

Benediction
```

Rev. A. D. King became pastor of Zion Baptist Church in Louisville, Kentucky, in 1965. In August 1968, A. D. Williams King became a co-pastor of Ebenezer Baptist Church. An installation banquet was held in his honor on November 4, 1968. The speaker at the banquet was his friend Rev. Leo Lesser Jr. (below left), pastor of Lee Chapel AME Church in Nashville, Tennessee.

Rev. A. D. Williams King envisioned the
need for the establishment of a children's
chapel at Ebenezer Baptist Church. In 1969,
Mary Manuel was chosen to develop the
chapel. Assisting Ms. Manuel were Carolyn
Searcy, Dodie Robinson, Laura Henderson,
and Nellie Demmons. Her successors have
been Christine Williams, Vivian Scruggs,
and Brenda Davenport. Ms. Manuel served as
director until 1969. Children's Chapel, now
the A. D. Williams King Chapel for Children
of Ebenezer Baptist Church, is open to all
children in grades pre-kindergarten to seventh.

Rev. A. D. Williams King Sr. developed the idea of a television ministry in the fall of 1968. The television station WAGA offered a 30-minute time slot for Ebenezer Baptist Church's programming. As a member of the Church Education Committee, Christine King Farris was asked to head the new effort. Mrs. Farris was eventually asked by WAGA to become the producer of the program.

```
            FORMAT - TV SERVICE FOR EBENEZER BAPTIST CHURCH

              To be Taped: January 15, 1969 - 7:45 P.M.
              To be Played: January 26, 1969 - 9:00 A.M.

        INTRODUCTION by Channel 5 Announcer


        Hymn No. 313 - Come Thou Fount ................................... Wyeth

        Call to Worship................................. Dr. A. D. Williams King

        Anthem - Sing Unto The Lord ............................ Van Dyke
                      Laura English, Soloist

        Invocation ............................... Dr. A. D. Williams King

        Chant No.527 - "Now For Each Yearning Heart" ............... Bigelow

        Responsive Reading ...................... Dr. A. D. Williams King

        Gloria Patri -

        Hymn No.335 - "Dear Lord and Father of Mankind" .............. Maker.

        Period of Meditation - "I Trust In God"  .................... Gabriel
                      Mary Gurley, Soloist

        MESSAGE  - "THE STANDARD OF GREATNESS" ...................... Dr. King

        Spiritual - "I've Been 'Buked" ............................... Johnson

        Benediction ............................... Dr. A. D. Williams King


        Sevenfold Amen
```

Initially, the stage was an improvised church setting, and church members brought with them some important objects, such as Ebenezer's pulpit. Later a set was developed for the program. The first program aired on January 26, 1969. This new ministry broadened Ebenezer's outreach and gave the church an audience that extended as far as Louisiana.

Obsequies

Alfred Daniel Williams King, Sr.

Co-Pastor, Ebenezer Baptist Church

Thursday, July 24, 1969

11:00 A.M.

Ebenezer Baptist Church

Dr. Martin Luther King, Sr., Co-Pastor

Atlanta, Georgia

The sudden death of Rev. A. D. Williams King Sr. was a grave blow to the congregation. The eulogy for the service was given by Dr. Benjamin Elijah Mays. One of those who gave tribute at his funeral was Rev. Leo Lesser Jr. who, only a few months earlier, had been the keynote speaker at Reverend King's installation banquet as Ebenezer Baptist Church's fifth pastor.

In 1971, the front of the Education Building was extended. Among the modifications was an interior stairway connecting the two buildings, giving members of the congregation access to the Education Building without exiting the sanctuary.

In June 1971, Rev. Otis Moss Jr. assumed the duties of co-pastor of Ebenezer Baptist Church. His official installation service was held on Sunday afternoon, August 8. The sermon for that service was delivered by Rev. J. A. Wilborn, pastor of Union Baptist Church. The charge to the minister was given by the Reverend Ralph D. Abernathy, and the charge to the church was given by Dr. Benjamin Elijah Mays.

The Otis Moss Chorale was made up of a collection of members from the choirs of Ebenezer Baptist Church. The fact that it was designated with Reverend Moss's name so quickly after he came to Ebenezer indicates the strong family spirit that existed within the Ebenezer congregation. In October 1971, the men of Ebenezer Baptist Church presented the Otis Moss Chorale in concert. The director and choirmaster of the group was Joseph A. Stephens. One of the soloists in the concert was Naomi King, wife of the Reverend A. D. Williams King Sr.

Ebenezer Baptist Church

407 Auburn Avenue, N. E.
Atlanta, Georgia 30312

Sunday . . . . July 26, 1970

COMMEMORATIVE SERVICES FOR

Rev. A. D. Williams King

July 30, 1930 - July 21, 1969

COMMEMORATIVE SERVICE
For
THE REVEREND A. D. WILLIAMS KING

THE SERVICE OF PRAISE

The Prelude—"O What, The Joy and Glory Must Be"---Matthews
The Call To Worship
The Processional Hymn No. 54------------God Of Our Fathers
The Invocation
The Chant------------------------------The Lord's Prayer
The Choral Worship--------------------Blessed Assurance

THE WORD OF GOD

The Responsive Reading No. 22-------"The Lord My Strength"
*The Gloria Patri
*The Hymn Of Praise No. 488---Mine Eyes Have Seen The Glory

THE EXERCISE OF CHRISTIAN STEWARDSHIP

The Presentation of New Members
The Announcements and Recognition of Visitors
The Offertory Appeal
The Presentation of Tithes and Offerings
*The Doxology

THE COMMEMORATIVE SERVICE

Tribute----------------------Deacon Arthur Henderson
Presentation---------------------------------July Club
The Altar Call----------------------It Is Well With My Soul
The Sermon-----------------------The Reverend Otis Moss
Pastor: Mt. Zion Baptist Church
Lockland, Ohio
The Hymn of Invitation No. 283-My Hope Is Built On Nothing Less
Benediction----------------------------------Rev. Moss
The Anthem---------"Hallelujah Chorus"---------Handel

"So Glad that Death Can Do Me No Harm"

MUSIC---The Church and Concord Choirs

MINISTERS OF MUSIC

David C. Stills   Joseph A. Stephens

The Sunday service on July 26, 1970, was a commemorative service for the Reverend A. D. Williams King. One of the choirs offering music for that service was the Concord Choir, organized by Alberta King in 1958 with 16 charter members. The choir was later directed by Joseph A. Stephens and then Myron Mundy.

In his recommendations for the 1968–1969 church year, the Reverend A. D. Williams King Sr. wrote, "In order to instill the idea of thrift in our members and reveal the concern of the church for the economic life of man, a committee shall be appointed to organize a Credit Union." It was during the tenure of the Reverend Moss Jr. that the Ebenezer Credit Union was established. In keeping with Ebenezer Baptist Church's commitment to involve the youth, young people were included in the operation of the Ebenezer Credit Union.

The Last Service Mrs King Played For.

June 30, 1974

Ebenezer Baptist Church

407 Auburn Avenue, N. E.
Atlanta, Georgia 30312
Church Phone: 688-7263

"Hitherto hath the Lord helped us"

MINISTER

Martin Luther King, Sr.

One of saddest days in the history of the church was the day that, as she finished playing the Lord's Prayer on the organ, Alberta King was shot and killed. In her book *Through It All*, Christine King Farris recounts, "At that instant, a young, bespectacled black man who we now know to be Marcus Chennault, who'd been sitting in a pew close to the organ, suddenly leaped to his feet shouting, 'I'm taking over here!'"

On July 2, 1974, Dr. Benjamin E. Mays, president emeritus of Morehouse College, delivered the memorial sermon for Alberta King held in Sisters Chapel on the campus of Spelman College. The following day, the funeral service included David Stills's arrangement of "Surely Goodness and Mercy Shall Follow Me" sung by the combined choirs of Ebenezer Baptist Church. The Reverend Sandy R. Ray, pastor of Cornerstone Baptist Church in Brooklyn, New York, delivered the eulogy.

Deacon Edward Boykin (right) was also killed, and two other Ebenezer Baptist Church members were injured. The shooter, Marcus Chenault, was a 21-year-old man from Ohio who claimed, "All Christians are my enemies."

Dr. Martin Luther King Sr. addressed the press after the murder of his wife. Pictured with him to his right are his daughter-in-law Coretta Scott King and Rev. Otis Moss Jr., former co-pastor of Ebenezer Baptist Church (Photograph by Boyd Lewis Jr.)

THE REVELATION SINGERS

presents

"HE'S EVERYTHING TO ME"

Elsie Knight, Sarah Ellis, James Jones, Joyce McCoy, Lena Haynes

3rd Anniversary Concert

May 27, 1979 - 5:00 P.M.

EBENEZER BAPTIST CHURCH
Auburn Ave. & Jackson St.
Rev. Joseph L. Roberts, Jr., Pastor
Rev. Timothy McDonald, Assistant Pastor
Dr. Martin Luther King, Sr., Pastor Emeritus

Elsie Knight went to the then director, James Jones, of the Martin Luther King Senior Choir and asked him to teach a trio of ladies "God So Loved the World." He agreed, and after a well-received debut in the second-annual Church Choir Memorial Concert in memory of Alberta Williams King, the trio became the M. L. King Sr. Trio—the original members all being from Ebenezer Baptist Church. The trio's first performance was in 1976. When Joyce McCoy, a member of Zion Hill Baptist Church, came to the group in 1977, the name was changed to the Martin Luther King Singers. In 1978, the group decided to change its name to the Revelation Singers. A group popular throughout the city and state, the spirit-filled Revelation Singers performed to a packed house in their concerts at Ebenezer.

The annual Ebenezer Church Choir Concert brought standing-room only crowds to Ebenezer. Part of the concert given on October 26, 1969, was the choir performance of "Four Freedom Songs." The four freedom songs were selected from eight "Freedom Songs" written by Thomas Merton in honor of Martin Luther King Jr. and the Christian nonviolent movement for Civil Rights. The music was composed by Alexander Peolouin. Coretta Scott King was the narrator for the performance, and the soloist was Matthew B. Fraling Jr.

EBENEZER CHURCH MINISTRY OF MUSIC

Presents

The Church Choir

In Annual Concert

SUN., OCTOBER 26, 1969   8:00 PM

DAVID CRAWFORD STILLS, DIRECTOR

JOYCE FINCH JOHNSON, ACCOMPANIST

EBENEZER BAPTIST CHURCH/407 AUBURN AVE., N.E.
ATLANTA, GA. 30312

REV. MARTIN LUTHER KING, SR., PASTOR

In November 1974, the Reverend Martin Luther King Sr. announced his retirement as pastor of Ebenezer Baptist Church. He recommended the Reverend Joseph Lawrence Roberts as his successor. Reverend King's dedication to the congregation is reflected in his book *Daddy King*, in which he writes, "It was time for me to retire from Ebenezer. My energies were not what they had been, and I did not want the church to decline under my leadership."

On Sunday, January 5, 1975, Rev. Joseph Lawrence Roberts Jr. was baptized by Reverend King Sr. Reverend Roberts had grown up in the African Methodist Episcopal Church. It was agreed upon by Reverend Roberts and Reverend King that Pastor Roberts would be baptized and join the Baptist church. Reverend Roberts's baptism brought national attention to the transfer of leadership of Ebenezer Baptist Church.

THE REVEREND MARTIN LUTHER KING, SR. SUNDAY

Ebenezer Baptist Church
ATLANTA, GEORGIA

"Blest Be The Tie That Binds....."

SUNDAY, JULY 27, 1975

Reverend Martin Luther King, Sr., Pastor
Reverend Joseph L. Roberts, Jr., Pastor-Elect

Sunday, July 27, 1975, was the day of the Reverend Martin Luther King Sr. Sunday program at Ebenezer Baptist Church. The plans for the day included the morning worship service and afternoon retirement convocation. Reverend King Sr. preached the sermon during the morning worship. During this service, he also passed the mantle to the incoming pastor, Dr. Joseph L. Roberts. The afternoon service included a number of tributes and music from the choirs of Ebenezer.

Three

NEW HORIZONS

Reverend Roberts Jr.
assumed leadership of
Ebenezer Methodist
Church on August 1,
1975. He was formerly
the director of the
Division of Corporate
and Social Mission,
General Executive Board,
Presbyterian Church
in the United States.

The Roberts family was welcomed by the Ebenezer Baptist Church congregation. Pictured here are Esther Jean Roberts (seated), Cynthia (standing left) Cheryl (center), Pastor Robert (standing right), and Carlyle (in Mrs. Roberts lap).

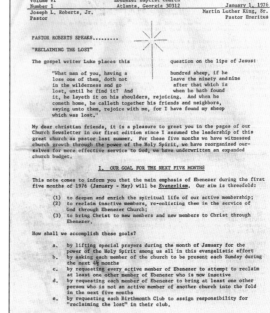

In the January 1, 1976, church newsletter, Pastor Roberts set forth his goals for five months of the year. In that same newsletter, it is noted that 75 members had joined the fellowship since August.

Ebenezer Baptist Church has a number of newsletters. The first newsletter was the *Ebenezer Messenger*. It was published by the Ebenezer Public Relations Committee of the Women's Council. The editors were Nellie Perry, Elise Gilham, and Esther Smith. The editor of the *Ebenezer Newsletter* was Malinda K. O'Neal. The third newsletter was the *Ebenezer Life*. The editor for that newsletter was Terrence Moore. In 2005, the *Ebenezer Newsletter* was renamed the *Horizon*.

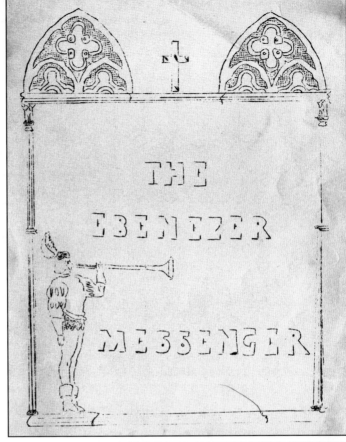

Ebenezer Life
A Look at the People and Events in the Life of Ebenezer Baptist Church

October/November, 1988   Volume 1 Number 1

Ebenezer men preparing for wonderful 'Day'

By Bryan Fortson

Men's Day, 1988 is coming. The date is Sunday, October 16. After a fruitful planning session in early September, which was attended by 78 brothers, the men of the church had their work well underway. The Men's Day co-chairpersons are Ronnie Davenport, Marion Allen and Godfrey Finch. If you are interested in getting involved with this special event, either as a participant or a spectator, contact one of the co-chairpersons.

Ebenezer's men have a wonderful lineup of speakers chosen solely for Men's Day. The 10:45 a.m. speaker will be Dr. James Melvin Washington of New York City's Union Theological Seminary. The Church will also be treated to some spirit-filled discussions from the Ebenezer Brotherhood's retreat which was held on September 11. These presentations will be made by Kevin Stacia during the television broadcast on the morning of Men's Day and by Carl Terry during the 7:45 a.m. service.

Regarding upcoming events, Henry Aaron, major-league baseball's all-time leading home run champion, will be the guest speaker at the annual Men and Boys breakfast on Saturday, October 8, at the King Center on Auburn Avenue. In addition, the spectacular J. L. Roberts Jr. Male Chorus will also be in concert on Sunday, October 9, at 5 p.m. in the sanctuary. Sponsors contributing $10 and patrons contributing $5 will have their names printed in the concert program.

All men are being asked to contribute $200 to the Building Fund for Men's Day. Your Men's Day captain

Marion Allen   Godfrey Finch   Ronnie Davenport

will contact you and explain this assessment.

The Men's Day effort is organized under nine committees: Donations, Finance, Publicity, Program, Music, Outreach, Membership, Catering, and Special Events. If you are a man in the church who has expertise in one of these areas, or, if you would like to learn, come to the Men's Day organizational meeting that will take place every Monday night in Fellowship hall until Men's Day. The meetings start with a light repast at 6 p.m., followed by a business session from 7 p.m. to 9 p.m. The Men's Day co-chairpersons have promised to stick to this schedule, and they've done just that. They've encouraged all Ebenezarians to be a part of this lean, mean, Men's Day machine.

Ebenezer men have selected five outreach projects. Three involve direct action. The men plan (1) to work with the residents of the Martin Luther King Village, (2) to bring coffee and donuts to workers at a labor pool, where those looking for day work can find employment, and (3) to aid a feeding program

Men's Day continued on 5

Male Chorus
audience widens

By Vivian Scruggs

The J. L. Roberts Jr. Male Chorus has experienced continuous growth and popularity since its inception in 1985. In addition to performing in several places around the Atlanta area, the chorus has performed in Michigan, West Virginia and Ohio. These performances include the singing of the national anthem at both the Atlanta Hawks and the Atlanta Braves games.

Group members will continue their trend of remaining extremely active with several upcoming performances. The third annual concert will be held on Sunday, October 9, at 5 p.m. in the sanctuary. This concert will feature music of black composers and spirituals. On the fourth Sunday in October, the Chorus will accompany Pastor Roberts as he preaches at the church of Reverend Ronald English, the son of Ebenezer's Deacon Jethro English, in Charleston, W. Va. On Sunday, November 6, Atlanta Falcons fans will

Male Chorus continued on 5

As ye have therefore received Christ Jesus the Lord, so walk ye in him: Rooted, and built up in him, and established in the faith, as ye have been taught, abounding therein with Thanksgiving. Colossians 2: 6-7

The Horizon

Volume 2, Issue 10   A Publication of Ebenezer Baptist Church   October 2005

Welcome Reverend Warnock to Ebenezer as our 5th Senior Pastor

Ministerial Staff

Reverend Raphael G. Warnock
Senior Pastor

Rev. Brenda Wallace
Assistant Pastor

Sunday Services
7:45 a.m. & 11:00 a.m.

Church Office Hours
9 a.m. – 5 p.m. (Mon. – Fri.)

Mission Statement
We proclaim and teach the liberating Gospel of Jesus Christ, for the purpose of gaining followers for Christ, who will share His redeeming love and power with all they meet.

407 Auburn Avenue, N. E.
Atlanta, Georgia 30312
(404) 688-7263
Ebenezer@bellsouth.net
www.historicebenezer.org

INSIDE THIS ISSUE

3   30 Years in Review

5   Esther Jean Roberts

6   Bulletin Board

7   Sick and Shut-ins

Reflections Of A Servant Pastor

As I reflect on our walk together over the past 30 years, the words of St. Paul to his dearest church at Philippi are so very appropriate. They help me express my gratitude to you, "*I thank my God in all remembrance of you, always in every prayer of mine for you all, making my prayer with joy, thankful for your partnership in the gospel from the first day until now.*" (Philippians 1:3) I thank our God for the prayers that surrounded us, lifted by you for Jeanine and me. We will always lift you up in our prayers.

We are so grateful to God for each of you, and for our walk together. It has not been difficult to be a servant leader in this place, because Dr. Martin Luther King, Sr. provided an excellent model of ministry, indelibly etched into our life together as a congregation. I thank God that while we all appreciate the great legacy of our past, you were open to new revelations for our future, which would enhance our witness and outreach. Thanks for your willingness to try new ideas and see new visions.

Ebenezer has always been bold and innovative. Proper process has always been secondary to Christian Purpose. Let us always remain this way, and always move in this manner. You have been so very creative and humbly serviceable in so many areas. This is a gifted congregation with people willing to share their individual gifts with others in need. You have been wonderful, volunteering as choir members, ushers, security team members, hospitality hosts to families after funerals, advisors to our youth organizations, and leaders of so many ministries...for this we are most grateful.

You have been open and receptive to me as your Pastor and Preacher. But more importantly you have taught me so much about walking by faith in times of darkness and doubt. You have been especially supportive in times of personal illness and loss. I have tried to be there for you in these times as well.

We have grown together through Bible Study Sessions, special study periods and retreats. We have participated in ecumenical worship and mission endeavors with other churches in our neighborhood and around the world. We have opened our doors to many people of good will, engaged in Christian witness, educational and cultural programs. We have invited the best preachers of our time, to this pulpit. They have enriched our lives. We have worked to develop a tithing church and to secure financial support for our endeavors in the larger community. I thank God for your work in ministry.

We thank God for the greatest music, musicians and choirs to be found anywhere! I am personally grateful for the way they have lifted our spirits to the throne of grace.

We are grateful to all who have contributed to the faithfulness and success of this ministry...to God be the Glory.

Now on a personal note...we are not going anywhere. You are our church family and we love you. We will support our new Pastor as he leads us onward and upward, just as you have supported us over these many years. Let us all join in unity and total support for our church's future.

Let me close as I began, (Philippians 1:3): "I thank my God in all my remembrance of you.... But now as a benediction we add, (Philippians 1:6) "*And I am sure that He who began a good work in you will bring it to completion at the day of Jesus Christ.*"

Thanks be to God for you all, and for the privilege of being God's under-shepherd and your Pastor these past 30 years.

Yours Always in Christian Love and Affection,

Joseph L. Roberts, Jr.

As the membership of Ebenezer Baptist Church increased and community outreach projects were expanded, Pastor Roberts chose Rev. Timothy McDonald as his assistant. He came to Ebenezer Baptist Church in 1978 after having served as the pastor of Shiloh Baptist Church in Dalton, Georgia. In addition to his preaching responsibilities, he was the pastoral liaison to the Christian Education, Community Outreach, and Membership Nurture Committees. McDonald is pictured below with his wife, Shirley. The couple became extremely active members of the Ebenezer family.

In February 1959, Willie Ponder was given permission by Martin Luther King Sr. to establish a committee to set up a Boy Scouts troop in Ebenezer Baptist Church. Later in that year, the church received authorization from Boy Scouts of America to establish the troop. Henry Griffin was one of the scoutmasters at Ebenezer Baptist Church at the time of its observance of Boy Scouts Sunday.

SUNDAY MORNING WORSHIP   **TEN FORTY-FIVE**

FEBRUARY 6, 1972

"BOY SCOUT SUNDAY"

THE SERVICE OF PRAISE

The Prelude————————"Dominus Rigit Me"————————Young
The Call to Worship:
    Minister: Search me, O God, and know my heart; try me and know my thoughts,
    Congregation: And see if there be any wicked way in me and lead me in the way everlasting.
*The Processional Hymn No. 54————————God Of Our Fathers
The Invocation
The Chant————————————————The Lord's Prayer
The Choral Worship————Let The Redeemed Of The Lord Say So

THE WRITTEN WORD OF GOD *Howard O'King*

The Responsive Reading No. 79————"Christian Influence"
*The Gloria Patri
*The Hymn Of Praise No. 263————————How Firm A Foundation

THE EXERCISE OF CHRISTIAN STEWARDSHIP

The Presentation of New Members —
The Announcements and Recognition of Visitors
Our Worship In Tithes and Offerings
The Anthem————"Let Not Your Heart Be Troubled"————Speaks
The Doxology

THE PRESENTATION OF THE WORD

The Meditation and Altar Call————————"Canaan"
The Pastoral Prayer
The Sermon————————————Reverend Martin Luther King, Sr.

THE RESPONSE OF FAITH

The Invitation to Christian Discipleship————Hymn No. 217
        Throw Out The Lifeline
*The Closing Hymn No. 27————————————Saviour Again
**The Benediction and Choral Amen
**The Postlude

    *The congregation stands
    **The congregation is seated

MUSIC FOR THE DAY

10:45 A. M.————The Church Choir
    David C. Stills, Director
7:30 P. M.————The Hymn Choir
    Mrs. Alberta W. King, Director

The Hymn of Praise . . . . **How Firm A Foundation**

How Firm a foundation, Ye saints of the Lord,
Is laid for your faith in His excellent Word!
What more can He say than to you He hath said
To you who for refuge to Jesus have fled?

-2-
"Fear not, I am with thee; O be not dismayed,
For I am thy God, and will still give thee aid;
I'll strengthen thee, help thee, and cause thee to stand,
Upheld by my righteous, omnipotent hand

-3-
"When through fiery trials thy pathway shall lie,
My grace, all sufficient, shall be thy supply;
The flame shall not hurt thee; I only design
Thy dross to consume, and thy gold to refine

-4-
"The soul that on Jesus hath leaned for repose
I will not, I will not desert to his foes;
That soul, though all hell should endeavor to shake,
I'll never, no, never, no, never forsake!"

TODAY IS BOY SCOUT SUNDAY In Observance of the 62nd Anniversary of Boy Scouts of America our Scouts are seated together this morning, along with the Scout Committeemen, the Scout Master, Dea. Henry Griffin and the Den Mothers, Mesdames Lucile Cooper and Jean Marie Waters.
    The Responsive Reading this morning will be read by Scout Bradford McWhorter.

NEW MEMBERS ADDED TO OUR FELLOWSHIP - JANUARY 30:
Miss Janice Hale (April) 755-1871
1250 Donnelly Ave., S. W #C-4

Mr. Joe L. Reed (Sept) 767-1076
1401 Holcomb Ave., East Point, Georgia

A WARM WELCOME IS EXTENDED TO ALL VISITORS TODAY AND ALWAYS.

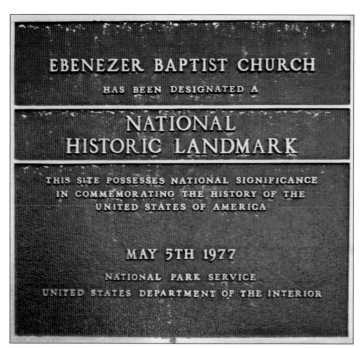

On May 5, 1977, Ebenezer Baptist Church was designated as a historic site as a part of the Martin Luther King Jr. Historic District. (Below courtesy of Boyd Lewis Jr.)

Rev. Sharon Austin and Rev. Edward S.
Reynolds were appointed as assistant pastors
in 1984, with Reverend Austin being
the first woman to serve in this capacity.
In 1992, they were elevated to associate
pastor status. Reverend Austin worked
primarily with the Christian Education
and Community Outreach Committees.
Reverend Reynolds worked with the
Stewardship and Membership Committees.

Because of the welcoming and supportive nature of the Ebenezer congregation, Pastor Roberts was able to open the pulpit to a number of young ministers. No fewer than 17 ministers who served Ebenezer Baptist Church under the leadership of Reverend Roberts now serve congregations of their own.

Sunday mornings at Ebenezer Baptist Church brought large crowds. Members and visitors from around the world packed the sanctuary—many to simply be in the place where Dr. Martin Luther King Jr. preached.

The Martin Luther King Jr. Week Annual Ecumenical Service has made Ebenezer Baptist Church a worldwide recognizable site. Presidents, kings, senators, governors, and national and international leaders have spoken from the stage where many outstanding ministers have spoken before.

In Celebration of the Fifty-Seventh Birthday Anniversary of
THE REVEREND DOCTOR MARTIN LUTHER KING, JR.
and
The First National Legal Observance of His Birthday by
The Government of the United States of America

King Week '86

EIGHTEENTH ANNUAL ECUMENICAL SERVICE

Monday, January 20, 1986
10:00 a.m.
Ebenezer Baptist Church

THE MARTIN LUTHER KING, JR. CENTER
FOR NONVIOLENT SOCIAL CHANGE, INC.

Jesse Hill, Jr.
Chairman, Board of Directors

Coretta Scott King
President and Chief Executive Officer

The year 1986 was truly a time of celebration for Ebenezer Baptist Church and the nation. Coretta Scott King's persistence was rewarded by the long-awaited recognition of the first national legal observance of Martin Luther King Jr.'s birthday by the government of the United States.

The banner above was placed in the vestibule of the Education Building to show the "New Ventures" proposed by Reverend Roberts. One of the projects with which Ebenezer Baptist Church was involved was the Atlanta Ministry with International Students (AMIS). AMIS encouraged friendship links between international students and Atlanta families and individuals. Ebenezer was one of five churches that served as sponsors of this program. Dr. Fahed Abu-Akel, an ordained Presbyterian minister, was the executive director of the ecumenical ministry. Below, a meal is shared with international students in Fellowship Hall of Ebenezer Baptist Church.

Men's Day has been observed at Ebenezer Baptist Church since as early as 1944, when Rev. Ralph Bailey was the speaker. Like Women's Day, Men's Day serves both a financial and spiritual purpose. Funds raised during Men's Day are used to support church projects. Activities prior to Men's Day vary from seminars on financial planning to group trips to a professional sports game. Mrs. King and Pastor Roberts greet the 1985 Men's Day speaker, Dick Gregory.

Annual Men's Day Observance

EBENEZER BAPTIST CHURCH
ATLANTA, GEORGIA

DR. BENJAMIN E. MAYS
Guest Speaker

Sunday   November 23, 1958

Dr. M. L. King, Sr., Pastor

The Youth Usher Board was reorganized by Mary Glenn in May 1983, with 25 members. For its first time as an organized body, the board ushered for Children's Day in June 1983.

As director of the Martin Luther King Sr. Choir, Clarence Robinson was energizing. Contemporary gospel combined with his own musical arrangements created an exciting musical experience for the Ebenezer congregation. This choir sponsors a concert each year in memory of Alberta Williams King.

The Martin Luther King, Sr. Choir
26th Annual Musical Tribute
In Memory
of
Mrs. Alberta Christine Williams King

"I'm So Thankful: A Celebration of Faith"

Sunday, June 25, 2000
5:00 p.m.

Ebenezer Baptist Church
The New Horizon Sanctuary
400 Auburn Avenue, Northeast
Atlanta, Georgia

Joseph L. Roberts, Jr., *Senior Pastor*
James E. Victor, Jr., Lisa D. Rhodes, Mary Finley
Assistant Pastors

Lanvester Jackson, *Director*

ORDINATION SERVICE

For

BROTHER VERNON CHRISTOPHER KING

Commit Your Work To THE LORD
Proverbs 16:3

Sunday - April 12, 1987

6:00 P. M.

Ebenezer Baptist Church
407 Auburn Avenue, N. E.
Atlanta, Georgia

Joseph L. Roberts, Jr, Senior Pastor
Assistant Pastors
Sharon G. Austin and Edward S. Reynolds

EBENEZER BAPTIST CHURCH
407 Auburn Avenue, N. E.
Atlanta, Georgia

ORDINATION SERVICE

Sunday, May 12, 1985
7:00 P. M.

Joseph L. Roberts, Jr., Senior Pastor

Assistant Pastors
Sharon G. Austin - Edward S. Reynolds

The Ordination Service

of

Sister Bernice Albertine King

Monday, May 14, 1990
—6:30 P.M.—

Ebenezer Baptist Church
407 Auburn Avenue, Northeast
Atlanta, Georgia

Joseph L. Roberts, Jr., *Senior Pastor*
Sharon G. Austin — Edward S. Reynolds
Assistant Pastors

The ordination service of a minister is a special and sacred one. Ebenezer has been the host of many ordination services for ministers who now have congregations of their own in Atlanta and throughout the country.

The women pictured here are, from left to right, Lillian Watkins, Sarah Reed, and Dora McDonald. Watkins and Reed were longtime secretaries of Ebenezer. They helped to maintain the smooth operation of the church. They were the "go-to" people for any information regarding the pastor's or the church's schedule or any other information regarding the church. McDonald was the personal secretary for Dr. Martin Luther King Jr. Visible in the background are some of the houses that were at one time across the street from the Heritage Sanctuary. (Courtesy of Sarah Reed.)

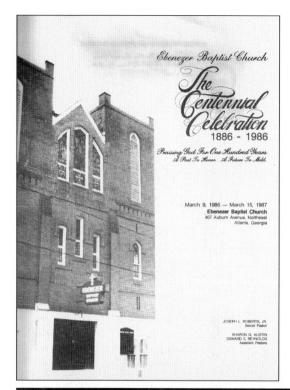

As Ebenezer Baptist Church approached its 100-year anniversary, the church embarked upon a yearlong celebration that included special concerts, a host of guest speakers, a dramatic performance, banquets, and other activities. The steering committee chosen to guide the year's activities was made up of, from left to right, Jethro English, Auretha English, Thomas Grant, Christine Farris, and Isaac Farris.

One of the activities was a march that followed the route that stopped at each of the four original sites of Ebenezer Baptist Church. The march went from Airline Street to McGruder Street to Bell Street and finally to Auburn Avenue. It was a spirited march that included a litany and prayer at each site.

The Men's Chorus at Ebenezer was formerly made up of a group of men who got together a few weeks before Men's Day to provide music for the day. After Men's Day in 1983, James Stovall agreed to continue to work with the group. Maurice Seay took over the Ebenezer Men's Chorus in 1984. The name of the chorus was officially changed to the Joseph Lawrence Roberts Jr. Men's Chorus in 1985. The spirit of brotherhood developed within the chorus provided the foundation for a strong commitment to the spreading of the glory of God.

Martin Luther King Jr. International Chapel
Morehouse College

welcomes

Ebenezer Baptist Church

EASTER, March 31, 1991
11 o'clock A.M.

Remember now they Creator in the days of thy youth, while the evil days come not, nor the years draw nigh, when thou shalt say, I have no pleasure in them; Let us hear the conclusion of the whole matter: Fear God, and keep his commandments: for this is the whole duty of man. For God shall bring every work into judgment, with every secret thing, whether it be good, or whether it be evil.

Ecclesiastes 12:1, 13-14 K.J.V.

THE OIKOUMENE FELLOWSHIP
VALUE CENTERED LEARNING
SCHOOL OF THE PROPHETS

On Easter Sunday 1991, Ebenezer Baptist Church was invited to participate in the morning convocation at the Martin Luther King Jr. International Chapel on the campus of Morehouse College. Examination of the back of the program revealed the name of Raphael Warnock as the president of the chapel assistants. Little did anyone know that 15 years later he would become the pastor of Ebenezer Baptist Church.

The Lillie Bell Memorial Usher Board was organized in the early 1940s with Barbara Low as the president and Lillie Coleman Bell as the advisor. As the members grew older, the original name of the board changed from Junior Usher Board to Young Adult Usher Board. In the 1950s, Malinda K. O'Neal took on the responsibility of advisor to the board. The name of the board was changed to the Lillie Bell Memorial Usher Board to honor the group's original advisor.

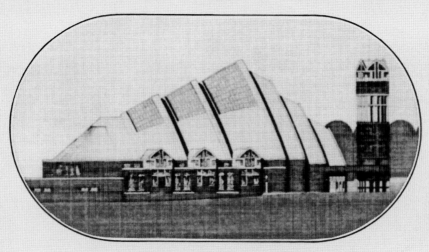

Ebenezer Baptist Church
407 Auburn Avenue, N. E.
Atlanta, Georgia

Groundbreaking Service

Palm Sunday, March 23, 1997
2:00 P.M.

The Reverend Dr. Joseph L. Roberts, Jr.
Senior Pastor

Assistant Pastors

The Reverend James Victor, Jr.
The Reverend Lisa Rhodes
Mr. Benjamin Carroll, Jr.
Mr. Latta Thomas, Jr.

The groundbreaking service for the new sanctuary was held on March 23, 1997. The chairpersons for the event were Jean Cooper, Leatrice Chapman, Alice Eason, Deacon and Mrs. Jethro English, Walter and Mary Hughes, and Ada Slocum.

The architectural firm of Stanley, Love-Stanley was chosen to design the Horizon Sanctuary. It is modeled after an African tribal meeting hut. On Sunday, March 22, 1999, Reverend Roberts led the congregation from Heritage Sanctuary to Horizon Sanctuary. (Courtesy of Aerial Innovations of Georgia Inc.)

The roof ribbing is reminiscent of African thatch. The bell tower is a weave-and-glyph-patterned obelisk. Placement of the Horizon Sanctuary on Auburn Avenue emphasizes Ebenezer's strong commitment to its urban mission to serve as a beacon of hope for all citizens of metro Atlanta. (Courtesy of Aerial Innovations of Georgia Inc.)

The National Parks Service leased what is now known as the Heritage Sanctuary. The church is now being carefully restored to its mid-1960s appearance and will be reopened for tours in 2009. Because of the historic nature of the church and the fact that it was a part of the Martin Luther King Jr. Historic District, the National Parks Service could better manage tours and maintenance of the site. While some special events will be held in the Heritage Sanctuary, the congregation has made the transition from Heritage to Horizon.

The Horizon Sanctuary accommodates approximately 1,600 people. The sanctuary is organized around fan-shaped seating sections with carpet, and seating resembling African textile patterns. The pulpit features custom-designed chairs, lecterns, and a communion table displaying African motifs. The configuration and openness of the building have made it possible for Ebenezer Baptist Church to accommodate a wider variety of events, such as the Atlanta Symphony Black Art Festival Concert.

The base of each interior column is clad with one of four African cross motifs. The tower edifices at Lalibela in Ethiopia were not built in the conventional sense but were hewn directly out of solid red volcanic rock. The Lalibela cross actually resembles an ornate, faceted square rotated through 45 degrees about its center. Priests carried hand-carved-wooden versions of this cross.

The cruciform depicts a cross with a centric circle at its representing Ebenezer as a "Church for All Nations." This represents a globe, which is symbolic of the earth and its nations. This was used on the main cross at the south narthex window wall and on the cross suspended above the communion table.

Beta Mariam is one of the four completely freestanding Lalibela rock churches. These rock-hewn churches are renowned for their window designs. This window was chiseled through the solid rock wall.

The Ebenezer cross is a part of the decorative grillwork in Ebenezer's Heritage Sanctuary in the choir loft's tonal opening. The strong Afrocentric flavor of this cross is reminiscent of the carvings on the Axum Stele in Ethiopia. Versions of this cross can be found throughout the Horizon Sanctuary and on the Bell Tower.

112

Chapel Music Company was chosen to design the organ for Ebenezer Baptist Church. David Stills served as a consultant for the planning, building, and installing of the instrument. The Alberta Williams King memorial organ is a large pipe organ augmented by a custom Rodgers digital console. The four-manual console controls the nine divisions of the organ with 162 stops and over 3,000 custom-scaled pipes. (Above courtesy of A. E. Schlueter Pipe Organ Company.)

The Alberta Williams King Memorial Organ Dedication

David C. Stills, Organist

Sunday, November 7, 1999 • 6:00 P.M.

Ebenezer Baptist Church

Horizon Sanctuary
400 Auburn Avenue, Northeast
Atlanta, Georgia

The Reverend Dr. Joseph L. Roberts, Jr., *Senior Pastor*

Shown here is the 2002 class of deacons. This class included the first women to become deacons at Ebenezer Baptist Church. The new deacons were, from left to right, Vivian Thomas, Duane Jackson, Ernestine Walton, Jim Gaskin, Ophelia Underwood, Kevin Sykes, and Deborah Shields.

With funds raised during the 1984 Women's Day Observance, a three-octave set of handbells was purchased. In September 1984, the Youth Handbell Choir was formed under the leadership of Cynthia Terry. In the fall of 1985, the Adult Handbell Choir was organized. Christine King Farris had been instrumental in the purchase of the bells, and it was decided to name the bell choir in her honor.

The 20th Anniversary Celebration

of the

Christine King Farris Handbell Ministry

"20 Years of Ringing His Praises"

Sunday, September 19, 2004
5:00 p.m.
Ebenezer Baptist Church - Horizon Sanctuary
400 Auburn Avenue, NE

Dr. Joseph L. Roberts, Jr., Senior Pastor

Mrs. Cynthia S. Terry, Adult Handbell Choir Director
Mrs. Sherri P. Jordan, Youth Handbell Choir

In 2006, after 30 years at Ebenezer Baptist Church, Reverend Roberts retired as the senior pastor. In the October 2005 issue of *The Horizon*, Ebenezer's newsletter, he wrote, "It has not been difficult to be a servant leader in this place because Dr. Martin Luther King Sr. provided an excellent model of ministry, indelibly etched into our life together as a congregation. I thank God that while we all appreciate the great legacy of our past, you were open to new revelations for our future, which would enhance our witness and outreach."

Four

A CHURCH FOR
ALL NATIONS

Ebenezer Baptist Church has a rich heritage of individuals who did not allow his or her goals to be limited by social mores or unjust laws. Ebenezer Baptist Church has had an ecumenical spirit that is not restricted to following strict doctrine but rather seeks to reach out to all those who love God, regardless of the denomination.

The church has been a haven for its members. It has been a house of learning, a source of support, and a place where leadership and life skills are honed to meet the challenges faced daily. Ebenezer Baptist Church has focused upon maintaining high moral standards while recognizing that forgiveness and grace are two of God's greatest gifts.

Ebenezer Baptist Church honors the memory of its past pastors through the upholding of the principles that they have all maintained—honesty, excellence, an unswerving faith in God, and a love for his or her fellow man or woman. It is based upon these principles that the congregation and the pastors have developed a strong witness for God in an urban community. A tradition of involvement of all ages in organizations of service, as demonstrated in the Women's Missionary Society (above) and the Mother's Board (below), continues to be a critical aspect of the Ebenezer Baptist Church mission.

Rev. Raphael Gamaliel Warnock began his pastorate of Ebenezer Baptist Church on October 1, 2005. His strong intellect, intense faith, and creative thinking has brought some innovative and groundbreaking methods of evangelism and outreach to the church and the community. Reverend Warnock's installation weekend included an installation symposium lead by Rev. Michael Eric Dyson, Ph.D., addressing "Poverty and the Faith Community: After Katrina." Sunday's installation was a wonderful blend of African tradition with traditional liturgical order. The preacher for Reverend Warnock's installation was the Reverend Calvin O. Butts III, pastor of Abyssinian Baptist Church in New York.

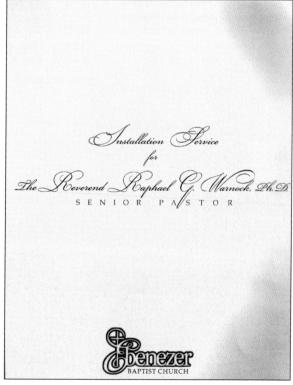

Installation Service
for
The Reverend Raphael G. Warnock, Ph.D.
SENIOR PASTOR

Ebenezer
BAPTIST CHURCH

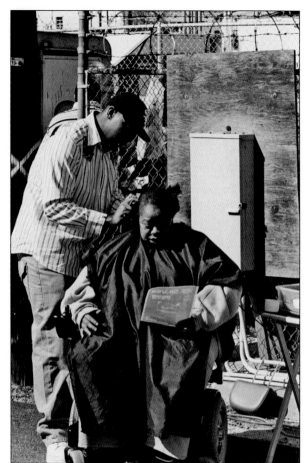

Outreach Ministry seeks to offer needed services or programs that connect Ebenezer Baptist Church to the community. Cutting through Crisis made available haircuts, food, and other services to anyone who attended. Events such as this help to make the church more accessible to the local community. (Courtesy of Vincent Bursey.)

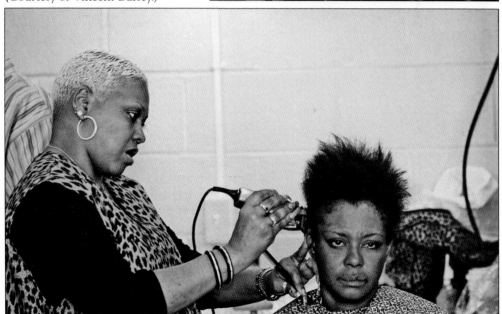

The Love Feast was first held at Ebenezer Baptist Church in the mid-1980s. It is a time when the church gives its Valentine's Day greeting to the homeless and needy in the community. A Valentine's Day dinner is served, and information is distributed regarding social services in the community. (Courtesy of Vincent Bursey.)

Special events like the Election Night "Watch Night" Service and the AIDS Awareness Service allow the church the opportunity to move toward "Victory in the Village," the theme and title of the outreach message of the church. Ebenezer Baptist Church continues to be a church where spiritual principles are put into social action. (Courtesy of Vincent Bursey.)

Ebenezer Baptist Church remains a mecca for those who embrace social justice and equality for all people. The mission statement of the church reads, "Ebenezer Baptist Church is an urban-based, global ministry dedicated to individual growth and social transformation through living in the message and carrying out the mission of Jesus Christ." Pictured in 2008 from left to right are Rev. Dr. Selina Smith, Rev. Dr. Raphael Warnock, Sen. Barack Obama, and associate pastor Shanan Jones." (Courtesy of Vincent Bursey.)

In the 119th-anniversary program of 2005, the following statement is printed: "Ebenezer has remained a church on the cutting edge of spiritual nurture and social change." This statement still holds true. (Courtesy of Vincent Bursey.)